Invoke The Elements

How To Use The Energies Of Earth, Air, Fire, And Water To Create Your Own Balanced And Intentional Life

Kristen L. King

Silvester And Eve Publishing

Copyright © 2022 by Kristen L. King. All rights reserved.

Silvester And Eve Publishing

6660 Delmonico Dr Suite D #326

Colorado Springs, CO 80919-1899

Design by Kristen L. King. Photography by Kristen L. King, Kenneth King, and Nathan King.

Cover illustrations licensed through Happy Watercolor Shop.

Internal illustrations licensed through the following: Happy Watercolor Shop, Aneta Design, Bloomella, MoshiClipArt, Abstractocreate, Winwin.Artlab, Elena Dorosh Art.

ISBN: 978-1-7336114-3-5

No portion of this book may be reproduced, distributed, stored, or transmitted in any form including photocopying, recording, or by any other electronic method, without prior written permission from the publisher or author, except as permitted by U.S. copyright law.

The advice and strategies found within this book are based on the experience and gathered knowledge of the author. This work is sold with the understanding that results vary greatly in every situation and are not guaranteed. Neither the author nor the publisher are held responsible for the results accrued from the advice in this book.

Download your FREE Elemental Energy Planner Pages and Tarot Card Spreads!

Plan each week so you feel your best every day! Use these FREE daily and weekly prompt pages to align with your intentions and create balance by planning the energetic activities, practices, and rituals that match the energy you need most in your life.

Go to:

http://authorkristenking.com/elementalplannerpages

To get your copy of the pages and start creating more alignment in your days now.

DEDICATION

For my children
May you always feel the rootedness of the trees, the freedom of the wind, the strength of the sun, and the flow of the tallest waterfalls. May life be a beautiful amalgamation of these elements within you, so that you never worry but always find your way back to the incredible energy within yourself to shift your reality, and see the beauty in all that you are and all that you can be.

Contents

Introduction	VI
1. Creating A More Balanced Lifestyle	1
Balance Mantra	27
2. Earth Energy	29
Stability Mantra	72
3. Air Energy	75
Wisdom Mantra	129
4. Fire Energy	131
Encouragement Mantra	168
5. Water Energy	171
Joy Mantra	207
6. Finding Your Own Proportional Balance	209
Alignment Mantra	232

Introduction

My life has had many cycles, and now that I'm turning the corner toward its fall season, I feel a strong sense of release. Through all of my career exploits, world travels, learning new skills, and growing a family, I always showed up as a striver. I am someone who continuously strives for more in their life so that I may continuously improve and evolve, but as I now feel myself growing tired of the constant pushing, I hear a new song playing in my heart. It's a song of letting go, of being free to feel the flow of the days and the whispers of my joy in the evenings. It's about embracing the moment I'm in and consciously being aware that those that remain should be met with gratitude and appreciation, instead of a search for the next thing.

Being a striver all these years has taught me I am so much more than I ever believed myself to be. I learned that getting out there and doing something big means you don't have to settle for what's right in front of you. The world is so much more expansive, and you have the power to be part of that larger expanse. As I've embraced life, I've felt the nervous excitement of quitting my job to leap at doing something for myself instead. I threw plans aside to make room for new, spontaneous adventures. I pushed past my comfort zone to take on new projects and delve into new areas of learning. I even faced my fears with unbelievable faith, forgiveness, and compassion. These instances showed me who I was at my core—a towering cliff standing tall amidst the crashing waves around me.

Being driven makes us grow, and that is the most fundamental part of life. However, we cannot do any of this without also having seasons of contemplation, inspiration, and rejuvenation. The seasons of life work together to give us the momentum for the growth we need. Without each of them, we'd drown in the tides of life before even making it very far offshore. So, looking back at the countless years I've spent striving for more, I thank my past self for all of the work that she put in towards her growth over many seasons of life without even really realizing it. I thank her for the late nights in the design studio, for saying "yes" to moving across two oceans, and for putting herself out there again after a loss that pulled many shadows into the light. From many of these experiences, I found the earth, air, fire, and water within myself and came to the point now where I can see how each played a role in my evolution.

Do I wonder what life would have been like if I hadn't pushed so hard most of the time? Do I question whether I needed to always be looking ahead instead of where I was at the moment? Absolutely. It might have been prudent to provide myself with more grace and be more fully present along the way. I could have been wiser about letting go of all the things that people told me I should do and just focusing on what my heart was telling me. Maybe I could have paid more attention to finding the joy right where I was and telling myself that the rest would unfold in time. But these are not regrets. Rather, they're the appreciation of the difference between my awareness at the time and my awareness in the present. I don't beat myself up for not spending more time being fully present instead of always setting future goals. Instead, I thank myself for the choices I made that allowed me to see things the way I do now and to have gone on the full life journey that I have had to get here.

My hope in writing this book is to show you that life balance is completely subjective and can exist in whatever form allows you to be your best self at any point. For you right now, it may mean spending your days immersed in work projects or family life. It could mean that you spend the weekends getting back to center and recharging your energy. In another five years, that balance could reset and lean you in another direction. Your life will have seasons, just as your years do. It's a natural part of living to go through these cycles and realize that nothing is permanent. The tides will change, and you will need to change along with them. The way you bring balance into your life today will look completely different from when you've experienced life more fully, challenged your viewpoints, and transformed into a more conscious version of yourself. Don't expect to get there overnight just because you've added more yoga into your mornings or more reading into your bedtime routine.

You will embody the seasons within your life over time, not all at once. As you see how the elemental energies are at play within you, you'll be much more capable of finding the balance setpoints that fuel your growth at each stage of your life. Be as mindful about the process as you can and show up with an open heart every step of the way. Acknowledge that every choice you make in life is the right choice for you at that moment. Every time you choose to stay late at work, take time to play with your kids, set boundaries with people, or even plan that once-in-a-lifetime trip, you are finding out more about who you are. There's growth happening there, which means that you're willing to become a better version of yourself. So, no matter what life looks like in hindsight, always be grateful to yourself for showing up and being willing to see what the next moment brings.

I wish you the highest vibrations on your journey forward. May you always come back to your truth and find your bliss in many moments along the way.

Feeling Complete

We are whole, whether seen or unseen
Dimensional in our truth
And abiding only by that which our soul dictates

Here in this space, it is not for us to see the boundaries
Where one aspect of ourselves begins and one ceases
But to know that all sides collide in order to remain one

For it's in that oneness where we find our authenticity
　The uniqueness that flows within us to express fully our genuine nature
　Being present to expand in our highest form, without restraint but only appreciation and love

aligning all elements

Chapter One
Creating A More Balanced Lifestyle

Time has taught me to respect where I am and honor whatever lies within me, requesting fulfillment at that moment. This lesson has taken me over hills and valleys of existence, swimming the depths of my soul for answers, and pulling myself out again to bathe in the sun's light. No matter the landscape of my life or yours in the past, present, or future, there is always beauty in the energy we approach it with. In that energy, we can move mountains, shift tides, and shine as much light as we need on our truth.

At this very moment, a few weeks after the New Year, I feel good after the holiday break, but it still feels like winter to me. Snow gently covers the ground around my property, and lightly dusts the mountains in the distance as I look out over the city. I know stepping into the New Year brings a lot of anticipation to head right into new goals and intentions. Yet, I'm perfectly content in the space that I'm in at the moment. For me, this is a transitional time to lean into the comfort of hibernation and stand still for longer before going full-force into all the things I have planned.

Years ago, I would have dove headfirst into the next extensive project, probably for my work, and given myself little time to appreciate the refreshing energy of the New Year before making a long list of tasks to complete. I would have set a bunch of deadlines and packed the calendar full to keep myself going full steam ahead and reach all of the expected goals. I would have been primarily concerned with my work, allowing for some time to relax on the weekends, but not much for my passions or anything else that truly inspired me.

It has taken half a lifetime for me to step away from that old version of myself and into a more aligned, harmonized version of me. I sit here now in my forties, feeling more content, more inspired, and more aware than I ever have been throughout my life after years of what felt like pushing a boulder uphill. I have now gotten to a place where I'm allowing life to flow more freely and I am moving along with it.

It's not a place I ever would have found myself in before, as I have always considered myself a type-A person. I'm someone who likes to be in control, to see where I'm headed, and to know that I've got everything to get me there with no roadblocks. But that's just the thing about life, isn't it? Control is just an illusion, and when we permit ourselves to let go of some of that control, that's when the magic happens. That's when we step out of our heads and into our hearts. That's when we feel free enough to follow what inspires us rather than the things that are expected of us. It's when we get to lose ourselves in the moment and find ourselves all at the same time.

When we hold on to the expectations of daily life and continue to go full-force all the time without really understanding why or what it's truly giving to us, we miss out on the genuine beauty of the journey. So, in the process of constantly striving and doing, we push against the currents of life just to get upstream rather than flowing with them to make things a lot easier and more enjoyable. In actuality, life doesn't need to be that hard. It doesn't even need to be about constantly pushing for the next thing to happen.

When you get comfortable with the cycle of life that you're in and where you are on your journey, everything feels so much lighter and more fluid than it ever has before. That's the best state to be in to feel more fulfilled with whatever you have in your life and to attract what you want in the future.

This is where cycles of life come into play. Here, in my sunroom overlooking the mountains, I'm leaning into a season of mindfulness. There's no rush to plan every detail of the coming months down to the hour. I'm not poring over how I'll make the next goal happen. In this moment, I'm appreciating the time and space where I am. I'm standing still to create moments of rejuvenation now until I feel motivated to create more growth. To facilitate real, transformational growth later, I need to make time now for awareness and peace.

When you live according to energetic cycles (that may or may not align with the actual seasons of the year), you give yourself more harmony in your mind, body, and spirit so you can achieve more in your life going forward. The days of living solely based around arbitrary goals and continuously striving for more keep you in a constant state of feeling like you never have enough. It puts pressure on you to always do more for your future. As a result, you will constantly feel as if you're lacking something. Maybe you will feel like you lack in what you have, what you have achieved, who you are, or what you've experienced. However, the lack only exists in your mind because you're approaching life from the viewpoint of constant momentum toward what the outside world expects of you, not what already lies within.

We want to change that and get you to a point where instead of continuously feeling like you need to be doing the next thing, you feel like you have the time and space to listen to your heart more and live from a place of heart-centered direction. Following a seasonal flow will ultimately get you a more consistent connection to what matters most and feels best to you at each moment in time. That's a really powerful way to live. Putting yourself in direct alignment with your most authentic self will change everything about how you show up in your life from that point forward.

First, I want you to take a moment to think about how much noise is around you as part of your everyday life. From the time you get up in the morning until you go to bed, how much are you inundated with conversations, news, problems, requests, and a million and one other things? It's hard to get any time to ourselves if we don't make it a priority to step away and create some space between us and the noise. If we're not careful, it can completely consume us, and we may end up resigned to it as normal in our lives.

Instead, I want you to reframe how you perceive the noise. How can you separate yourself from it and be more of an observer? When we get so caught up in the noise, we experience a need to be immersed in it. As a result, we continue with the hustle of life around us to maintain the sense of tracking alongside everyone else, if not edging further ahead. But what if that is just an illusion? There is no reason to keep up with anyone else because life isn't a race. Life is more of a progressive journey that each of us must uniquely take to find peace within ourselves.

If you thought about it, would your idea of success realistically be the same as your neighbors? It's most likely not, but so much of the time, we don't even slow down to check in and see what would feel good and successful for us. So we just move through our lives tallying up the checkmarks to keep up with other people's expectations, judgments, and the obligations we feel toward them. Likely, we also push ourselves based on our own judgments and expectations of ourselves, which makes us lean toward saying "yes" to quite a few things that deep down we probably would rather say "no" to instead. Sound familiar?

Breaking this habit of pushing through life based on the pace that the outside world sets for us is something that we must do in order to live a more meaningful life that makes us happier and more fulfilled every day. If you can't hear your own wants and needs above everyone else's, then who will suffer because of that? You will, as you'll be unhappy with how you're spending your time and energy. Besides that, though, you won't be giving your best energy to the people and things around you, and they'll end up feeling that. However, when you can show up from a place of inner strength, clarity, self-love, and inspiration, you bring more joy and positive energy to your days and the days of everyone you interact with.

So in order to be a happier, more aligned, and abundant person, you don't have to push constantly to check that next box or to keep up with the people next to you. Work on how you are showing up to honor what most aligns with your energy and your intentions. That doesn't always mean spending your time doing self-care rituals or reading a bunch of books. It could mean making plans to follow one of your passions, or at other times, connecting with people in a heart-centered way. The good thing is that the more conscious you become about your own energy and the season of life that you're in, the more you'll be able to balance out how fulfilled you feel and how much growth you've achieved.

Let me just tell you that in the forty years I've spent pushing that boulder uphill, I've had my fair share of stressful times. We lived overseas with a newborn baby at a time in my life, and I remember being close to my breaking point. I definitely felt like a struggling new mom, and my husband was gone most of the time to make matters worse. Plus, I was trying to run a blogging business from home and run the household, so everything seemed to fall on my shoulders. I would wake up several times a night to feed the baby, get up super early to keep him on schedule, take care of the house, and start my work whenever I could squeeze it in. Without fail, there would always be some crisis that occurred while my husband was gone, whether it was something breaking around the house, a military issue that had to get sorted out, or a category four hurricane coming straight for us. It was up to me to take on everything and keep it all together while I kept my head on straight and also figured out how to achieve my own goals.

To say that time was exhausting would be an understatement. It honestly sent me straight to the edge of my sanity, and I really did not know how I was going to move forward from that point. I couldn't see past the constant busyness and stress. To keep my head above water, I was just in a constant state of hustle that I couldn't seem to pull myself out of. It was as though I couldn't ever catch my breath before more tasks piled on top of me. I didn't ever really enjoy that season of my life, even though it was a time that I could have been appreciating every moment with my new son. It was quite the opposite, really. As my baby cried for hours on end, I would cry right alongside him, feeling like nothing in my life seemed to fit. I couldn't seem to get to a good place with my energy where I felt strong, happy, or even successful.

I wanted so much in those moments to throw my hands up and give up because everything seemed like it was pushing against me, no matter how hard I tried to keep it all together. Nothing seemed enjoyable, and all I could think about was how miserable it all felt and how I just needed to keep plowing through it as best I could. I was thinking about the house to-do list, the goals that I had made that weren't getting done, the type of mother I wanted to be but I didn't feel I was living up to being, and all the other mounting pressures.

When you're in a place where you're living up to expectations set by yourself and others, you're always living from a lower vibration. You spend your time and energy on what the mind tells you to be appropriate or necessary, and you leave behind the feelings of the heart. This is a closed-off space that doesn't allow you to open up to the beauty that is present in the moment. Instead, you become stuck in a cycle of frustration over everything that's happening "to" you in your life rather than "from" you. Shifting this perspective was one of the biggest transformations that helped me move out of a constant uphill battle to a point where I could see myself as a driver of my own life.

Once I did this, I was no longer living based on the world outside of me dictating my next steps, how I would spend my days, or even how I showed up in my life. For once, it gave me the ability to see that my internal energy and intentions were what would allow me to reshape my life into exactly what I needed. They were what would drive more fulfillment for me rather than living based on outside forces. When I finally got that, everything became lighter, and I finally could rearrange things in my life to where I no longer pushed that boulder uphill. Instead, I gradually let go and found a more peaceful way to move along my path.

Soon, I spent more time on personal development to get to know myself better, what I really valued, and what felt satisfying to me. I still had many goals and aspirations, but I was managing them more from a place of personal awareness and satisfaction and less to get ahead and achieve external success. I started building in time to reflect more on my mindset and energy so that I could reframe what wasn't working and move past what was blocking my growth. It was a time of profound shifts for me, all while becoming a mother for the second time and moving back to the States to start fresh.

So my life had underlying seasons already built into it, but whereas before I was too stuck in the weeds to see how I could move with those cycles and appreciate them, now I was identifying how I could create my own seasons of energy and a life that felt much more freeing and balanced. It was just a matter of removing myself from the noise around me so that I could allow my inner guidance to kick in and set the tone for my life instead.

START WITH YOUR HEART

Before I get into what it means to live in these seasonal flows, I want to touch on a couple of key foundational ideas. First, most people live their lives by following their heads. They think of things in the practical sense of getting things done, managing the logistics of their lives, and checking all the boxes that will help them achieve the "right" things to give them measurable success. This leans heavily on the masculine energy that we all have within us. It's geared toward the drive and motivation you have to take action and achieve things in life. While this is a natural and necessary part of us needed to accomplish anything in our lives, it's also only a part of the equation.

We need to pay more attention to another side of ourselves if we're going to create a life that feels more soulfully aligned and fulfilling for us. That side is the feminine, and it's really about being more open to your emotions, passions, and intuition. It allows us to be much more connected to whatever we're doing and receive a sense of abundance from our lives. This aspect of ourselves can get lost in the very hurried, task-oriented society that we live in. So we must find the time and space to recultivate this energy within ourselves and use it to harness our potential for a bountiful life.

The first step in doing this is to open your heart. Give yourself a chance to let go of all the what-ifs, the shoulds, and the have-tos, and instead take some time to feel into things. This may be uncomfortable at first if you're used to thinking through things logically or approaching life from a practical perspective. I encourage you to embrace this concept because it'll get you a lot farther than you ever could go using just your masculine energy alone.

There's a reason that even CEOs and business leaders are now focusing on leading from a much more intuitive standpoint. Your inner guidance already knows the way ahead, and when you open yourself up to listen to it, the best opportunities follow. We can't perceive all of the incredible abundance waiting for us from our minds alone. Life isn't always logical, and we have to be emotionally perceptive enough to follow the signs. That means first being willing to receive the nudges and intuitive downloads that hint at the right path to give us our greatest gifts along the way.

Being open to receiving means first opening your heart. You can do this with a few simple steps. Let go of whatever is in your mind and tap into your heart chakra. Focus on something that makes you feel love, compassion, or deep gratitude. Allow yourself to feel the thankfulness you have for those things in your life, and pay attention to how that makes your energy feel through your mind, body, and soul.

Imagine that your heart center is opening and light is pouring out from it more fully with each thought of gratitude. As you do this, allow more light to extend from you and create more space in your heart center for even greater light to enter.

Now, it's time to set an intention. The idea is to be more open to what life offers you in terms of love, connection, inspiration, abundance, and anything else that you seek. All you have to do is to be willing and available to receive what life wants to give without closing yourself off to it. Tell yourself that you are ready to be guided to create a life full of joy and fulfillment. You are ready to come out of your head space and embrace the cycles of life through a lens of heart-centered awareness and alignment. This intention will not only draw your attention to the power you yourself have in finding the most meaningful things in life, but it will also show the universe that you can see your life journey as a gift to be received and that you're ready for that gift to open up to you.

When you open up your heart center, you also increase your awareness to make more aligned decisions. You elevate your perspective enough to see that you are not at the whim of life moving around you. The currents may move swiftly, but you'll no longer get swept up in them unless you choose to do so. As we'll discuss in later chapters, water is an incredible energy of flow, and as you discover it within yourself, you'll be better able to find strength in the movement of life and how you intentionally react or flow with it.

There's one other thing about opening your heart center to prepare for as you start this journey. When you open up to what lies within, the world becomes more complex and yet much simpler. You see your complex inner world much more for what it is: the driver of your reality. With that comes a deeper acknowledgment of your underlying beliefs, fears, desires, and whole truth. It can be a lot to process through this, but on the other side of opening up to this comes honest rebirth into a more whole and authentic version of who you're meant to be.

On the flip side, life becomes much simpler when you open up. You see everything around you for the white noise that it is. The daily grind loses its appeal, and you see the world in a state of constant reaction to stimuli that you no longer have any interest in chasing. It's possible to peel back the layers to see what truly has meaning for you and which pieces will support you in living a more connected, intentional life. Those are the ones that will attract your attention, and focusing on those few key components can activate your highest level of being.

BEING MORE INTENTIONAL WITH YOUR TIME AND ENERGY

So you've opened your heart, but now what? Well, in order to establish more meaning in your days and in your life holistically, it's important to begin with intention. Your intentions are what should drive everything you do all the way from the momentary actions that you take to the larger, long-term decisions you make. When you have really clear intentions, then life becomes much simpler and more fluid.

Looking deeper into the meaning of intention, we can identify it as a deliberate direction for your efforts. It's assigning a purpose and value to something before doing it. In this way, everything has a "why" that drives you forward and gives you a much firmer foundation to build your plans, decisions, and actions. In his book, *Think Like A Monk*, Jay Shetty says that "Without a reason for moving forward, we have no drive. When we live intentionally — with a clear sense of why what we do matters– life has meaning and brings fulfillment. Intention fills the car with gas."[1] Living from a place of intention brings you into your heart center and establishes your inner emotions as the root from which everything else stems. This way, you're releasing the need to live according to outside expectations, judgments, and obligations because you're first checking in with yourself and what feels most meaningful to you. That's where the fuel sparks a motivation within us.

Intention gives you the ability to have more alignment with your personal values, and brings you back to your inner power and wisdom for how you whole-heartedly want to live your life. It's a natural way to establish more confidence in yourself, what you're doing, and where you're headed without being swayed by others. "To live intentionally, we must dig to the deepest why behind the want. This requires thinking not only about why we want something, but also who we are or need to be to get it, and whether being that person appeals to us."[2] You can always check in with your intentions to clarify why you've chosen one thing over another and know that there is a method to your madness. It's very reassuring and comforting, and we really need that grounding effect when we get into our heads about whether something is best for us.

Now having this intentionality should flow into all aspects of your life, not just with setting certain goals. Everything you do can have intention, and by creating that meaning for every piece of your life, you shape the reality that gives you the most joy, alignment, and connection. Of course, usually we're only thinking about this in terms of what we want in the future, like a lovely house in the perfect area of town or starting a family and having a beautiful life together. That forward-thinking intentionality is only a piece of the puzzle. It's up to you to bring more of this into your life in the present moment as well, so that you can more fully experience happiness along every point of your journey.

This was where I was during that time overseas with my newborn son. I wanted so desperately to have time to focus on my future goals and to make those a reality that I was missing what was right in front of me. I was drowning in doing all the things and frustrated with not achieving all the intentions I had for the months and years ahead. The feelings of being stuck and inadequate in the present only grew as I attracted more of the same energy.

I lost my intentional focus on the present moment and that made me miss the incredible gifts that I had right where I was. Things like spending a lot of time with my baby when he was so young should have been a blessing, but to me, it felt like a struggle at that moment. That meant that I wasn't paying attention to what I needed in my life in order to feel like myself. I disregarded my need for self-care and gave myself very little time for creative inspiration or anything that would rejuvenate my soul. As a result, those moments felt like I was clawing my way through life when, in actuality, I didn't need to see them that way at all.

Being aware of your energy during each cycle of life can be the difference between feeling completely stuck and frustrated with your situation and allowing yourself to embrace moments of joy that can provide exactly what you need to feel whole. As you understand how to tap into the energetic seasons you're in more fully, you'll be able to create more specific intentions to live by in the present and for the future you'd like to create. Both are necessary for a well-lived life, and both will allow you to feel more at ease with whatever comes your way.

So when I talk about being intentional throughout this book, I'm referring to having a heart-centered reason for doing something that feels very aligned with your energy. This will bring you more connection with where you put your time and energy so that you're not missing a chance to take care of yourself, seize an opportunity, or enjoy your life fully. Let your energy be your guide, and your heart can then produce the intentions. With this flow, you'll be approaching every day, every season, and every year with a beautiful viewpoint of self-awareness and compassion for not only yourself, but for others and life as well.

FINDING THE ELUSIVE IDEA OF BALANCE

For many, the idea of creating balance in their lives is a complete myth. They reject the idea that having balance is even possible and ignore the possibility in favor of just plowing through life by whatever means necessary. For others, balance is a continual quest to find an equilibrium. It always plays in their minds and guides the decisions they make. So which viewpoint is valid to live life to the fullest? Well, that really depends on you, but I'm guessing that if you're here, you're leaning toward the camp that would like to find more harmony in their life.

The thing is that balance really can be a myth if you look at it from a certain perspective. If you think that you have to be doing a little of everything and spreading yourself between many aspects of your life all the time, then you're most likely going to find burnout rather than balance. However, you've got an opportunity to reframe how you look at creating harmony in your life. Instead of seeing it as evening everything out in terms of your time and energy, you could choose to look for what works for you and realize that it will change repeatedly. What may feel like a great balance one day could be totally out the window the next.

Nature shows us this regularly. Some days the sun shines brightly, the birds gather for their nests, and the world is at work from dawn until dusk. On other days, there may be six hours of partial sun. The trees slowly release their leaves in the waning daylight hours, and the world gradually finds its way inside more hours than not. There isn't just one way of creating balance. Sometimes it takes leaning more heavily on one side of the scale to feel in alignment. It's not always an even exchange of energy between equal parts. The same is true for you. You are not all equal parts of the energies within you and the dimensions of your life. With each passing day, you'll have to decide whether you must lean a little heavier on one side than the other or if you must release something to lighten the load.

Overall, we each have a setpoint that will feel right for us. Maybe for you, that setpoint will be a significant focus on family, with a much lesser role being played by career and creative pursuits. For your best friend, it could be completely different. She may find that her best setpoint leans more toward enhancing her mind, body, and spirit while tangible things like career and finances play a much lighter role. Finding your balance is a very personalized process, and it's not something that you can set once and forget. It's an evolution that coincides with the journey of who you are. It requires us to check in with ourselves regularly to adapt, change, and grow more fully into a more aligned version of ourselves, becoming more aware over time.

To say that we can achieve balance by just setting up a few routines or blocking off our schedules suggests a lack of awareness of the overall goal of life: intentional presence to grow into the fullest expression of ourselves. With this in mind, balance has a purpose, and it's something that we need to cultivate through our own awareness of who we are and our place in this world. It's not just about recognizing a need to have more quiet time. It's an endeavor to support your soul to be the best it can be at every point in your life. So in order to show up most fully and create your best life, it requires you to do the work to find your own version of balance. It asks that you seek the parts of yourself that want to flourish and enhance them through the other parts of yourself that compliment your intentions.

Throughout this book, I'll be showing how you can tap into the different energies within you in order to balance the whole. You get to decide which ones are most calling to you now and which ones you may need to incorporate better into your life regularly. I'll show you how to embrace every aspect of yourself so that you no longer feel like one has precedence over any other. And then, I'll bring it back full circle to give you the best ways to find your own setpoint for a fulfilling, abundant life. Your journey to achieving balance won't look the same as anyone else's, but it will come from an authentic place that propels you forward and provides exactly what you need to grow into your highest self.

THE FOUR ELEMENTAL ENERGIES WITHIN YOU

Now that we've discussed intentionality and balance, let's focus on the four elemental energies you can draw upon to create more fulfillment in your life. We all have masculine and feminine energies that we can tap into based on what we're trying to accomplish. These energies are meant to be in harmony with one another. Yet, when we dominate our lives with too much of one, we can feel unbalanced and start having issues with our growth. Perhaps we aren't sure of the right path and don't take any action at all, or maybe we're checking so many boxes that we don't stop to check if we're really fulfilled.

The masculine and feminine support us in feeling inspired and aligned with our soul's desires, and in achieving all that we're meant to create for ourselves in life. One without the other will only produce half the results we're looking for in life, if that. Yet, when we learn to lean into seasons of masculine and feminine energy that best support us in our intentions, that's when we have a recipe for an incredible path ahead filled with growth and deep fulfillment. So we use the four energetic cycles of earth, air, fire, and water to tap into the specific masculine and feminine aspects we need to propel us forward in living our best lives.

We can approach this by using the corresponding seasons of the year to align with these energies, or we can create our own cycles based on when we most need them in our lives. Combining both approaches best ensures that we spread these energies throughout the year and allow ourselves to incorporate them at set times and when it suits us. This ensures that we'll tap into both masculine and feminine energies at some point and derive the most benefit from each. Depending on how you currently feel about different areas of your life, you may shift things around and take advantage of longer cycles for some things and shorter cycles for others once you understand what's lacking and what you've got plenty of already. Don't feel you need to stick to set timeframes for any of this. Everything is an opportunity to see what feels most expansive for you and give you whatever you're looking to enhance in your life.

Plan on giving yourself some time to process each of the elemental energies, though, and really understand how they can support you. We're going to go through each one so that you have a complete understanding of the impact of bringing that energy into your life. Remember, these energies are part of nature, and so are you. They all live within you just as all of nature experiences these cycles as well. These seasonal cycles are how everything balances itself out and creates growth and progress. Nothing ever stays stagnant for long. It all continues to go through cycles of change and evolution. What we want to do is to mirror these seasonal energies in our own lives so we may also grow and evolve.

You'll see that the elements of earth, air, fire, and water correspond to the natural seasons of the year. Spring, summer, fall, and winter each have an element that embodies the spirit of that season. By choosing the cycle of energy that feels most natural and good to you, you'll move fluidly with the changing currents of life, appreciate where you are, and still be in control while shaping the reality you desire. As you gain a deeper awareness that everything is happening at the right time for you, you'll also see your growth follow periods of rejuvenation to allow for greater transformations.

So as we move through each elemental season, approach it with an open heart and an open mind. Set your intentions for that season based on how you feel you need to fill your cup to correspond with that energy. When your cup feels full, you'll feel expansive, vibrant, and like you're standing in your power with moments of joy and complete connection with your highest self. Everything will feel truly supportive, and you'll feel a deep sense of gratitude for those moments. If something feels misaligned, take a step back and ask yourself where you're at with this energy in your life right now. Try to pinpoint the specific areas that need attention and focus your intentions around those. Your intuition will always be your guide throughout this process, so remember to check in regularly with your gut feelings and what your body is instinctually telling you you need.

WHAT YOU'LL GET OUT OF THIS PROCESS

Living in seasonal cycles is about finding a more intuitive path to personal growth and development. It's also about being more deliberate with what you need to feel your best concerning your mind, body, and spirit at each point in your journey. Doing this has some incredible benefits that you'll find as you create these cycles for yourself. For instance, you may experience a sense of ease in your life and look at things through a lens of personal priorities and values. You may find a great deal of clarity and awareness about what truly makes you happy and what you can let go of, which can create a great deal of freeing energy within you. Plus, there's the fact that you will be more in tune with your inspiration and passions. This way, you can develop more plans and projects that align with things that light you up and take action on them with confidence and motivation, knowing you're being guided to things that bring you genuine joy.

On top of those incredible benefits, the actual opportunity here is that you have the chance to bring more happiness and abundance into your life, starting right now. As you set your intentions and live in these cycles to do more of what brings you joy, you'll find your perspective on life opening up. When that happens, you become a magnet for more beautiful things to find you. The universe will respond to the higher energetic vibration you're living by, and it'll realign things to work more in favor of what you desire. So the abundance you've been looking for will now become increasingly attracted to you and make its way over to fit nicely into your life. This all happens because you step out of the lower level vibrations of stress, frustration, stagnation, and perhaps even competition. Instead, you balance your chakra energy centers through these cycles, and create more expansion in the higher level energies that will open you up to work with life rather than against it.

Remember, these can be tremendous shifts, depending on where you currently are in your life. It may take a lot to sort through what you need and get your cup filled back up to the level it needs to be at to create all of this abundance. However, if you pay attention to yourself, go within to find more of the answers that you need, and allow yourself to find more joy and gratitude in the moment you're in, then you will reap the benefits as it all comes together. This is the time to start so that you'll be closer than ever to your most aligned, harmonized life.

HOW TO BEGIN

Before you dive headfirst into the elemental energies and start rearranging everything, it's best to begin right where you are. Get a sense of what is actually going on in your life right now so that you have a bit of an inventory of what is working and what isn't. It's best to give yourself a bit of space and some reflection time to figure out where you think adjustments need to be made. In doing this, you'll gain insights into where to direct your attention first.

I recommend asking yourself how full you feel your cup is in the major areas of your life, including self-care, health and wellness, finances, inspiration and creativity, relationships, leadership and career, personal development, purpose, spirituality, and recreational enjoyment. Gauge what your heart is telling you about what each of these areas feels like now, so you can identify which areas may be intentional focus points as you head into each season of life. For instance, if you feel like health is something that you need to work on, then you may choose to connect with your physical body through the earth energy of winter and also do some more active pursuits through the fire element of summer. By gauging your current reality through what your heart tells you is lacking or is full, you'll have an intuitive metric as a starting point for your journey.

The other thing I want you to pay attention to as you begin is whether you tend to lean toward your masculine or feminine energy. We each have a natural default energy that we steer toward. When you know which one it is for you, you'll be more aware of balancing that out when you're feeling like things are out of alignment. Say, for instance, that you are a very goal-oriented person who is always planning out what you should do next and making sure you stay on track toward your goals. Then, it would be incredibly important that you pay attention to ensure you don't get too burnt out by overloading yourself with tasks or never taking time to rest and replenish your energy.

We'll cover ways to do this in the upcoming chapters, but for now, just get a sense of your natural setpoint in terms of energy and how you typically approach your life. Use your intuition to take those reflective moments and decide what is and isn't working, and then set some priorities around where to bring in more of the energies you're lacking. At first, this could bring up some discomfort or resistance for you, but that's a good sign. It means that you're hitting a nerve, and that's something that needs a bit of attention, which we'll cover later. The more you dig into those areas and incorporate them into your life piece by piece, the easier it'll get and the more centered you'll become.

I'd also like to suggest that during our energy discussions, whenever you feel like developing some rituals or practices in your life, take that as a good sign you're being drawn to that energy. It's holding your focus for a reason, and by incorporating it into your days through ritual, you'll integrate it more fully into your lifestyle long term. So don't be afraid to test out different practices and how you can fit them into your schedule. You're bound to find a few things that really work for you and give you a more substantial way of pulling those energies into your intentional lifestyle.

You're on the verge of transforming your life to have profound meaning for how you show up, connect with yourself and the world around you, and approach your days with more clarity, confidence, and ease. Using these seasonal cycles can harmonize all the pieces of your life and provide the intentional lifestyle that you ultimately want and need. So be sure to open your heart fully, connect with your inner guidance, and just allow yourself to be led on this journey one step at a time. The energy within you, surrounding you, and aligning for you is about to change.

Life Design Action Steps
Getting Started

1. Practice setting intentions for how you regularly use your time and do so by connecting each action or activity with the meaning behind it.

2. Ask yourself what your personal definition of balance is at this point in your life and how you may or may not be living in alignment with that definition.

3. Reflect on your natural state of being and whether you lean more heavily toward masculine energies of determination, structure, and leadership or toward feminine energies such as creativity, emotion, and inner connection.

4. Determine if there are certain areas of your life that you'd like to work on first or whether there are spots that feel any lack, discomfort, or resistance that need to be addressed.

---

1. Shetty, Jay. (2020). Think Like A Monk. New York: Simon & Schuster.

2. Shetty, Jay. (2020). Think Like A Monk. New York: Simon & Schuster.

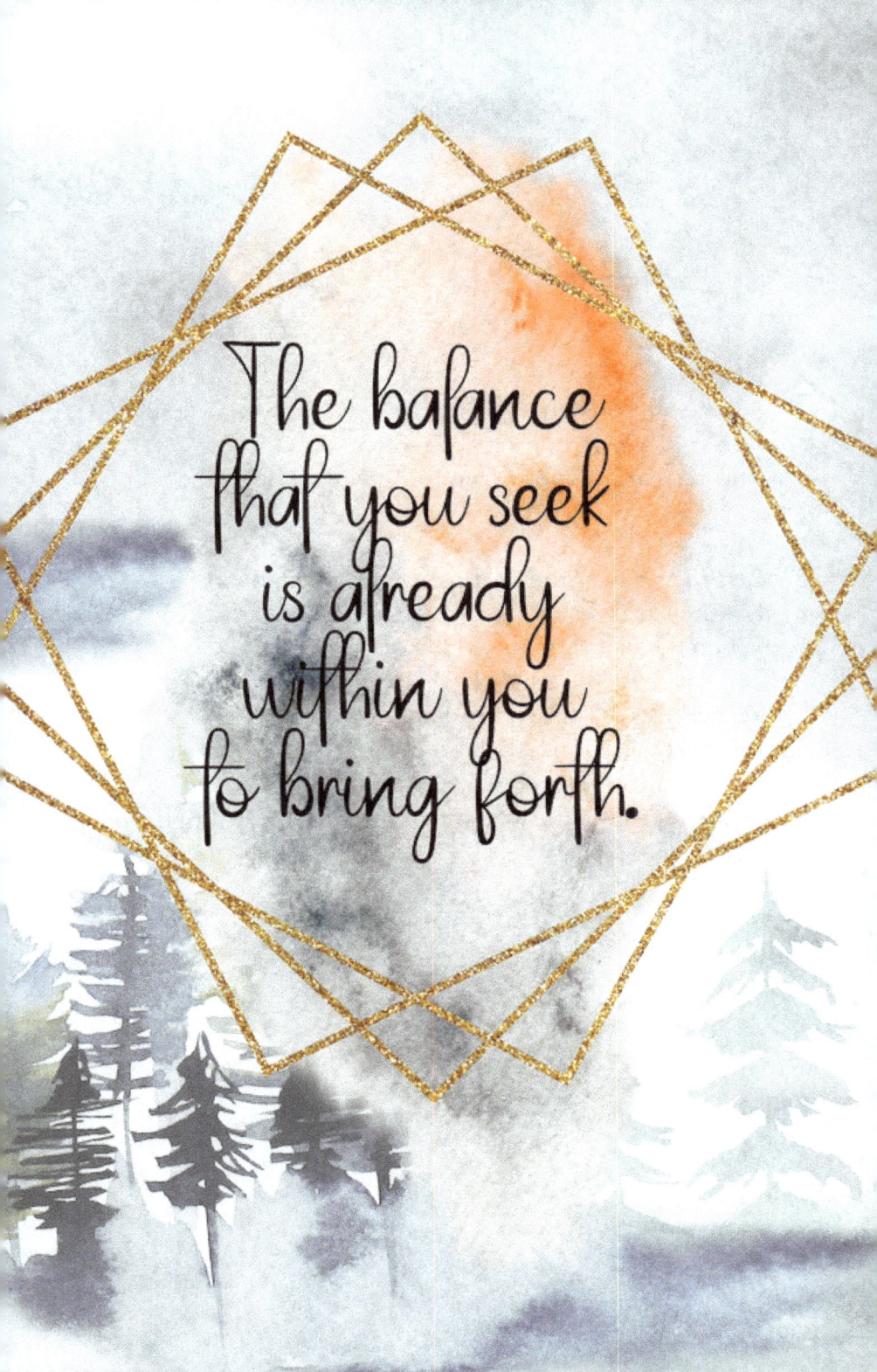

Submerge yourself into the darkness of the longest nights
Allow the world to melt around you
And retreat into your own mind with thoughtful reflection

Be still and hear the beatings of your own heart
For they are what will whisper to you the path ahead
When the days renew and life begins again

Yet for now, it's time to rest and unwind
Connect with your soul and deepen your bond with the earth
As we move into the winter that recovers our strength and roots us solely to what is

Chapter Two

Earth Energy

Have you ever felt that deep sense of groundedness and support from connecting to nature? It's like no matter what is going on in the world, you can go out for a walk in the garden or a hike up in the mountains, and your energy will completely transform. This energy flows within us, and when we tap into it, we can create a stable, affirming sense of self-awareness that keeps us steady on our path. That is the power of your connection to the earth.

Think about the archetype of Mother Earth. She is nurturing, and provides some stability and support for all that she cares for. We thrive because Mother Earth cares for us by giving us food, water, and all that we need to survive. These basic needs give us strength and help us elevate into higher areas of growth, since we know the earth satisfies our foundational requirements. When we talk about these fundamentals of our physical existence and what we inherently need to feel supported, we're referring to the energy within us at the root chakra. This is the point from which everything else stems.

If we do not first take care of our physical selves, then we cannot move on to our minds and souls to raise our consciousness beyond the physical. It's the absolute, most basic piece that sustains us. So to continue our personal growth journeys and keep moving to the next level, we must be mindful of how we're nurturing the earth energy within us regularly. This means honing in on our physical well-being and doing all the things that will bring us back to center, ground us, and support us in clearing out all other distractions.

The best way to do this is by being present. Coming into the present moment and noticing where you are will bring you a strong sense of groundedness. It'll take you out of your head, where we so often live our lives, and put you back into a place of just becoming an observer of the moment. The value in this is that we can dispel a lot of the distractions, fears, expectations, and chatter of the "monkey mind," that primitive nature in us to overthink everything. As we do this, judgment melts away, and we can much more easily see life for what it truly is, rather than what our minds and the rest of the world are feeding us about it.

In moments of mindfulness, we can go within and reflect on a much deeper level than when we're surrounded by the busyness of life. This practice then becomes very supportive and self-nurturing. It not only gives you a chance to rest, rejuvenate, and connect with your physical body, but it also provides a chance for the renewal of mind and spirit as you retreat away from the noise of the world. Your thoughts become your own, and you have the space to receive more awareness about what the next level of growth should be for you.

The key to stepping into this earth energy within you is to recognize that all things must pause to have the strength and stability for a new season of growth. Before beginning any new endeavors in life, everything must have a season of rest to first build up the stamina for that growth process. Consider how in winter, which is the season of the earth, many parts of nature go into hibernation mode. The trees and plants lie dormant with bare branches, pausing any new growth until they've had a chance for a reprieve. Animals go into their homes and find cozy nooks where they may rest and conserve their energy before another cycle of life ensues. This is life's moment to pause, and to have the energy to continue our developmental process fully, we need to accept this as a necessary time to rejuvenate our strength in mind, body, and soul.

Now, I know for many of us, the idea of taking a break to step away from the hustle of everyday life is a hard pill to swallow. We can't possibly wrap our heads around how to take a moment away because if we do, it'll all pile up and feel worse than before. Yet, it appears and feels that way because we've allowed ourselves to get caught up in the expectations and pace of a world that is not based on what we necessarily control or value. We're living for other people's limitations of our time and energy and putting ourselves within the confines of a reality we didn't intentionally create. When it gets to this point, we give our power away to the world and choose to live according to the life guidelines set by others.

It becomes even more imperative to take a step back and come into your earth energy when you feel like this. Doing this is the starting point from which everything else along your journey will stem. It will give you the space to return to your center and honor your inner guidance above all else. You'll feel more vibrancy for life after a period of rest. You'll see that your decisions are your own in how you show up in your life, choose to spend your time, and connect with the world around you. You'll be better aware of how to balance your energy and detach from the noise of life, and you'll find a deeper sense of gratitude for where you are in your journey.

So as you think about how you may integrate this earth energy into your life and create cycles to support you in this, be mindful of what you're trying to cultivate here: restorative peace and reflection. This isn't the time for action plans or big trips to meet friends. It's time to pull back, find some easeful moments, and give yourself space for contemplation and rest. It's okay if you're uneasy about this at first or if you take a while to work this into your lifestyle. The point is that you become aware that this cycle puts you more in the driver's seat of life for the other seasons to come. In no other cycle will you have the chance to remove yourself from what's happening around you like you do in the earth cycle. Take this as an opportunity to experience a sense of self without everything else pulling at you. Embrace it as a gift that allows you to feel almost born again in certain instances when you need that rejuvenation most.

Now, you need to have a solid understanding of how you can integrate earth energy into your life. We'll walk through the importance of mindfulness, what it means to practice going within, how you can keep yourself grounded and centered, and the integration of gratitude into your life. When you put these pieces together, you'll have an incredibly powerful toolbox of practices that will enable you to feel more supported, stable, and inwardly connected as you move throughout your life. This is all work that will balance out your root chakra energy and give you the foundation you need for growth. All you need to do to get started is clear out all of the noise and distractions around you and be willing to find a bit of tranquility within yourself.

THE IMPORTANCE OF BEING PRESENT IN THE MOMENT

It was late in the evening, and the winds were howling around our home in Okinawa. The storm was right over us, sitting and staying a while, unwilling to move on just yet. The hurricane winds were no joke, but I knew our sturdy concrete house could withstand the pressure. Of course, that didn't mean that the rattling front door didn't worry my mind and keep me from going to bed. I kept my eye on it regularly between thoughts of the door flying off its hinges and the wind summoning all of its strength to sweep away everything in the entry.

Then, there was the thought of how soundly my little one would sleep that night. With my husband away again, while I was alone in the hurricane with our baby and the unsettled cat, I knew it would be a long few days and nights. The constant rapping on the windows of the blowing leaves and branches and the whistling of the persistent winds would wake us every so often from whatever sleep we could manage. The baby would have difficulty going down, and I would battle all night to ensure that the air conditioning went back on after frequent power outages.

It was a nerve-wracking time, feeling alone and yet having so much to care for at the same time. I did everything I could to get out of my head, be present, and know that everything was alright. We were safe and sound in our house, and although the storm outside was wreaking havoc on the island, I could be sure all was well inside the house. So I did what I could to barricade the front door and check that all windows and doors sealed up nicely and tightly. I soothed the baby to sleep for the first time that night. Then I climbed into my bed with the cat, to focus on the cool sheets on my skin rather than the raking noises outside the window.

Now, we had many hurricanes on the island in the time that our family lived in Okinawa, and eventually, it became commonplace for us to hunker down inside and ride out the storm with more ease. Yet, I remember that storm being a more intense one. The winds were stronger than I had experienced before, and I had yet to see the front door shake and flex like it had with that storm. It heightened my emotions as I was taking care of our baby boy on my own that time, and I needed to ensure that he felt more comforted and secure than anything else. I also knew that I had to let the storm pass around us and just focus on the stability that I could create within.

I had to find little ways to let go of the stress of the outside storm. It didn't matter that I would most likely be awake in a couple of hours with the beeping of the air conditioners telling me the power was out. I did my best to not think about how the cat would restlessly walk over me all night, notifying me of how I, too, needed to be on guard. For those moments, I would ground myself in the sensations of that soft bed. I would let my head touch the pillow and focus on how all was well inside the house. I would appreciate the chance for some much-needed rest before the little one awoke to the screeching branches or the need for a midnight snack in the middle of it all.

That storm continued to rage for a couple of days. Through it all, I remained grounded and secure inside with the cat by my side and the little one doing his best to be indifferent to all the clatters and howls that didn't affect him all that much at all. Those moments during hurricane season, though, made me press pause on life. They made me see it was necessary to have these clearing cycles where life came to a halt so that we could get fully present for a while. It was necessary to separate ourselves from the storms around us to find stability and strength within ourselves. Plus, it was important to find our way out of our heads sometimes and just know from within that all was exactly as it needed to be.

Mindful moments can be pretty powerful if we use them to anchor us into moments of strength and stability. For me, when everything feels like it's in utter chaos, the best thing I can do for myself is to step back, breathe, and get my head on straight before heading back out there. Otherwise, it's just too easy to get thrown around in the middle of the instability. However, coming back to yourself with mindful moments gives you the chance to find more clarity, objectivity, and higher awareness so that any further decisions get easier, not only in times of stress but also every day of our lives.

Practicing mindfulness gives you the ability to achieve a higher energetic level of connection to yourself and the universe in any moment so that you feel that inner sense of support. From there, you can receive more insights internally about the next steps or how to proceed once you ease back into life. Essentially, you do this by reducing the immediate intensity you feel from stressful stimuli and instead become more of an observer for a while. You come out of your head and just experience the present moment for however long it takes to anchor yourself in a sensation of stability.

For example, perhaps instead of spinning over how to solve a certain problem, you instead look at what's right in front of you and pinpoint one minor item that deserves your attention first. Rather than feeling the stress of all the bills piling up, you could instead draw your attention to one specific person you work with who truly values your skills and abilities enough to pay you what you're worth. If your kids are really pushing your buttons and you can't seem to lower your frustration with them, you could shift your awareness to creating some quiet moments for the whole family to do individual activities that bring you peace.

Start getting used to the idea that your attention doesn't always have to go toward the past or the future. The present moment deserves your time and focus more than anything else because that is all there really is. You exist in the present moment, which is what we have right now. Getting good at honoring that will reduce the stress that comes from the "what ifs" and the "should haves" and put you back into a place of empowerment for what is possible right now.

Let's talk about how to do this easily. First, you want to become an observer and look at the present moment objectively rather than subjectively. Take your thoughts and emotions on overdrive out of the equation for a moment and give yourself a chance to see what's happening. Become still and tap into your senses. What do you see, hear, smell, taste, and tangibly feel? What can you describe that you're experiencing right where you are? This practice allows you to detach from all the mental clutter that constantly keeps you spinning, and draws you into a more grounded position of awareness.

This provides space for you to regroup and create some sort of separation between you and the perception of all that "needs to" or "should" occur. Give yourself a minute of pure existence outside of judgment, and just "be." Here you can focus on breathing, get more tapped into your senses, or even focus on an extremely logical task, such as counting or measuring. Any of these things will bring you into the present moment and push all else out of your mind for a bit of time while you regroup.

You can also practice mindfulness for more extended periods of time. For example, it works well when you are experiencing something with people you love or doing an activity that fulfills you. Just imagine that you are pausing at certain instances of the experience to take mental pictures of the scene to capture it as an observer. This could be while you're doing anything from baking cookies with your kids to hiking up a mountain for the first time. See the motions you are going through as if you're looking in from above and trying to identify all the details, highlights, and the scene as a whole. Draw your awareness to certain aspects of what is going on, and let your focus fall on whatever attracts you most in those moments.

The peacefulness comes in not trying to force these moments to be anything. You're just gaining a higher level of consciousness around what exists without having to justify or understand anything in your mind. This is purely about connection to the experience itself, and as a result, you'll gain an empty mind. It's in that space of an empty mind where internal guidance may then arise, and you can observe more about yourself mentally, emotionally, physically, and spiritually. Then you notice your present self in all you are and all you can be. That's the connection that we want to get to through mindful moments.

MINDFULNESS EXERCISE

Take a few moments to sit quietly and observe your breath. Put your hands over your belly and feel it rise and fall with each inhale and exhale. Mindfully follow the flow of the air as it comes in through your nose, into your lungs, and pushes out your belly. Hold the inhale for five counts and then exhale with a sigh. Pay attention to your belly falling with the exhaled breath. Practice this breath awareness for a few more cycles.

Then notice the way your body feels right where it is. Draw your focus to the bottoms of your feet and how connected they feel to what is below them. Feel the energy moving up through your legs, into your torso, your arms and hands, and up your neck and shoulders to the crown of your head. Imagine the energy running through your whole body connecting with a rich red glowing light. The earth below you grounds that light through the bottoms of your feet. Allow this connection to support you and give you a sense of stability. You are grounded and deeply connected to the energy of the earth. Let this energy flow through you and give you the awareness that you can move through life with strength.

Now, allow that red energy to dissipate and move back into the earth below you. Feel your body being soothed and comforted. Draw your attention once more to your breath and your hands on your belly. Take a deep breath with gratitude for the stability and strength within you, and exhale as you finish this exercise.

WHAT IT MEANS TO GET GROUNDED

Often when we talk about tapping into your earth energy, we're referring to getting grounded. This is the most fundamental piece of mindfulness where you come out of your head, firmly plant yourself in the present moment, and become aware of your physical body and senses. That may be in relation to your breath, whatever you're touching, what you can see, or whatever else you may be experiencing.

Drawing your attention to your senses makes things very tangible in the moment. So if you've been feeling like you've been juggling too many ideas in your head lately, getting grounded will give you a chance to let go of all of that for a moment and focus on reality. It will make you aware of what you know to be true in that moment rather than focusing on the what-ifs in your mind. This is the tangible nature of our presence here on earth as well. We are experiencing a physical reality, and even though we interpret it in our minds, we can always come back to the definiteness of what exists right before us.

Do you know the saying that someone is "up in the clouds" and needs to come back down? Well, it's referring to when someone is stuck in their mind thinking things through too much instead of being present for what's happening or what's down on the ground. Sometimes it's necessary to remove ourselves from the clouds and return to what's happening to feel a greater sense of stability. Think about how you feel when you daydream. You probably feel you're in another world for those moments and lose track of everything around you. That can be what it's like when we get lost in our minds from worry, stress, fear, or anxiety as well. Those emotions take us away from what is happening right before us. They can cause us to spiral into a lack of clarity and control over our lives if we're not conscious of it.

In order to bring ourselves back to a state of calm and acceptance, it helps to find grounding practices that anchor us to reality. The best way to do that is through our physical presence. So we use our surroundings and tangible activities to create physical awareness. When you go into nature, for example, it's highly likely that you become very in tune with what's happening around you. Perhaps you smell the scent of the pine trees in the air, the coolness of a lake on your skin, or see the multitude of colors showing up in the fall leaves. These stimuli bring your attention to what exists, not what may or may not come to pass. What you are experiencing is what is already available to you, without question. It's real, and it can comfort us as we interpret those things as facts in our minds and immerse ourselves in them through our senses.

Therefore, one of the best grounding practices you can use is to immerse yourself in nature. Get outside and go for a walk. Plant some flowers. Go for a swim or go down to the lake and watch the birds fly overhead. These activities will connect you to life as it currently exists. When you do this, you can also appreciate how connected you are to that Mother Earth energy we discussed. You are on this earth right now, and it gives you what you need. Getting outside to experience it will remind you of that fact, and you may not feel so distant from your true nature.

Besides getting in touch with nature, there are so many amazing activities that will enliven your senses. Perhaps some of them are already your favorite hobbies and pastimes. For instance, playing sports or even doing craft projects gets you in touch with your physical body and what you're doing with it. Whether running the bases to get a home run or threading a needle to stitch a quilt together, you are engrossing yourself in the physicality of those tasks. Each time you go through the motions, you bring yourself closer to the awareness of your present self. So everything else will melt away in order for you to concentrate on those actions.

You can also try being more mindful of tasks at home. Cooking, baking, loading the dishwasher, doing the laundry, or even opening mail, although not the most engaging of activities, can help you get out of your head and focus on mundane tasks that bring you down to the present moment. Just think about doing the dishes for a moment. It's not something that you have to think too hard about, be creative with, or even communicate well in order to do it. You're just placing one dish at a time into the dishwasher trays, and you need to be fully present to identify which dish, cup, pot, or silverware piece goes where.

The act of organizing and grouping items allows you to hone in on exactly what you're doing in that moment. You're really just going through the motions and applying logic most simplistically to accomplish one very tangible task. Now, if that doesn't pull you into reality, you will likely need a much bigger break to clear your mind.

Let's walk through one more example, though, with cooking. Cooking is a direct representation of earth nourishing and providing for you. This is great if you'd like to bring in elements from the earth to support you in grounding. There are so many layers that can go into this, from growing your own vegetables in the garden to simmering lots of beautiful aromas together for hours on the stove. It's also an amazing practice for getting in touch with all of your senses. Plus, it's incredibly easy for all of us to bring this activity into our lifestyle because we need to eat every single day. Just the pure acts of cooking and eating will give us a connection to our physical bodies.

So I want you to think of some ways that you like to ground your energy and feel a direct connection to your body, your environment, and the present moment. Make a list to refer to in order to incorporate these activities more regularly into your daily routine. Become accustomed to taking a few moments to focus on your breath more often and see how that feels to you. There are no wrong ways to get grounded as long as you're doing your best to "come out of the clouds" and bring more attention to your present reality. The more you do this, the better you'll be at stepping away from stress created in your mind and finding your way back to a calmer state of being.

CENTERING YOURSELF

Just as you can create a more stable energy for yourself through grounding, you can also do this with centering practices. They basically go hand in hand with grounding as they both bring you back to yourself and what you know to be true in the present moment. For centering, though, it's more inwardly focused on you. When we looked at grounding, we focused on the environment around us and how they were being perceived through our senses to give us that feeling of stability. With centering, it's more about taking time to identify your own truth at the moment. That includes doing things that make you feel like yourself in the fullest capacity possible.

For instance, you may have people asking you to commit to a million things, but all you really want to do is focus on one activity that means the most to you. So you could remove yourself from all of those "asks" and return to center by focusing on the one thing that makes you feel whole and fulfilled. Basically, it's about finding security in what makes you feel like your most authentic self. If that means that you know you most love creative time, then maybe centering consists of painting, taking photographs, or pulling out some adult coloring books when you're feeling tossed around by everything around you. It could mean that you feel really connected to music, so spending some time listening to your favorite songs allows you to breathe easier and feel more at peace.

Centering allows you to revive your sense of self and know that no matter what is happening around you, you can always return to the truths you know about yourself to feel stable. Ask yourself, what traits do you know to be true about who you are? Maybe you know you are kind, responsible, determined, or creative. Affirm those things you know to be true so that you will regain a sense of self-empowerment that may feel lost after any interactions in the world. You can use experiences you've had or even things that others have told you to affirm this for yourself and regain acceptance of your authentic self.

Then, you'll want to bring the energy you've devoted to everything else around you back to yourself. Focus on shaking off everything that has asked for your attention. Whether it is work, children, social commitments, or anything else, visualize drawing your energy back toward you and centering it into your body to reestablish a sense of wholeness. Reconnect your spiritual self with the physical by envisioning your entire being recharging and filling with brilliant energy. Through this practice, you energetically return to your center and allow what was being drained from external sources to feel whole again.

So as you take time for activities and visualizations that bring you back to your sense of self, you can use these with the grounding exercises. They'll both help to connect with both your outer reality and your inner reality consistently. Both require regular maintenance to know that you are strong and supported right where you are. One without the other may make you feel "off," as though you don't quite feel rooted to where you are in life, connected to reality, or in control over your energy and where it goes. So by bringing activities from both sides into your lifestyle, you'll be activating your highest potential for connectivity to your present reality.

GOING WITHIN

As you withdraw and take moments to stabilize your energy, you'll also be able to go within yourself more and create the quiet you need to hear your inner thoughts, feelings, and guidance. This may take a bit of practice to get used to if you have done little meditation or inner work before, but the more you do it, the more clarity you'll receive. The basic idea is to come into a state of greater oneness and presence with yourself. The to-do lists get set aside. Put everyone else's requirements on the back burner, and give yourself moments where you reflect inward.

You can do this in many ways, so try out a few different practices and see what suits you best. To begin, set an intention for what you hope to receive or allow as part of your time going inward. Spiritual guide and author Gabrielle Bernstein says, "Through the power of your intentions you can reorganize your energy in an instant. Remember that your intentions create your reality. Power lies in knowing how your positive presence expands your outer life."[1] Sometimes you may just set an intention to clear your mind and reduce stress. Other times, you may have a deeper answer that you're seeking about which decision to make, what path to take, or how to show up more fully in your life. Then, there are also times when you're going within to uncover the depths of your soul and go deeper into things that may hold you back or keep you stuck in your life. No matter your intention, hold space for your practice.

Open yourself up to receive higher guidance for your greatest good when you go within. Once again, it's through openness that you will receive the most profound and aligned insights. They may come from your higher energetic self, spirit guides, or the universe itself. Regardless of the source, the awareness is all within you, just waiting for you to tap into it and start listening. When you do, the answers to your intentions will become more apparent.

Dr. Joe Dispenza, author of *Becoming Supernatural*, recognizes the difference going within can make in establishing clarity that can change our lives. He states, "If we focus on the known, you get the known. If you focus on the unknown, you create a possibility. The longer you can linger in that field of infinite possibilities... the more you are going to create a new experience or new possibilities in your life."[2] Stillness has the effect of bringing in new insight as the space is no longer filled with noise. You have the opportunity to push everything out of your mind and just become available to the truth that lies within you, letting it come to the surface to bring messages for your next cycle of growth. This is what we're hoping will emerge from us through going within.

To practice this, you can choose activities such as meditation, journaling, quiet contemplation, creative mindfulness such as coloring or photography, or even mind/body exercises such as yoga. Set your intention first. Take a few moments to ground yourself and connect to the present moment. Open yourself up to receiving insight. Then go through the motions of your chosen activity, immersing yourself in the experience. Allow your thoughts and feelings to flow naturally, but continue bringing yourself back to your original intention. Focus your energy on that one intention and imagine you are sending it off into the universe so that it may message you back with what you need to know.

You may choose to use soothing music or nature sounds, surround yourself with crystals, burn some incense, or diffuse some essential oils to create a space of tranquility for your energy. These things will support you in gently clearing the energy and guiding your focus inward. It's perfectly acceptable to do this in brief spurts and then work up to establishing an entire routine around going within. The key, though, is to let go of everything else around you for however long you can. Even just giving yourself a minute to regroup in the middle of a hectic day at work will pay dividends in your mental clarity and emotional state throughout the rest of the day. So don't be afraid to start with the easiest way to implement this into your life and work your way up to a practice that feels good to you.

In terms of the insights you can expect from going within, there can be many things that you may gain from doing this. Depending on the intentions that you set, how open you are to receiving insight, and the amount of external noise you're able to distinguish, you could very likely have some answers come to you in the same session. Other times, you may need to sit with a question or intention for a while before gaining awareness. That is to be expected, especially when we're in our heads and have difficulty detaching from our constant thoughts. It takes time to send an energetic intention out into the universe and then have clarity come back to us in a way that we can identify and understand.

Be gentle with yourself in this process, and know that working through things internally isn't always easy and quick. You may need to journal your thoughts and feelings until you uncover the actual issue of what's holding you back. You may find a solution to something you're struggling with in the form of a friend making a comment. Insight could also come about when you're in the middle of a yoga session and finally have the "ah-ha" moment you're looking for. Be willing to give that awareness time to percolate and come back to you in whatever way it needs to, because there's no right or wrong way for clarity to manifest. All you need to do is become an open vessel for receiving that clarity and know that by taking these steps, you are allowing yourself the best chance of success.

Now I just want to reiterate the importance of going within. This process is the precursor to all of the other work you'll do in the coming seasons towards growth. Without cycles where you allow yourself to step back and gain awareness, you'll be too scattered and overwhelmed that you won't be able to make meaningful decisions that are best for you. Going within will essentially clear the mental and energetic "decks" before you load any more onto your plate. This way, you'll feel refreshed and stable first and have a much stronger awareness of what is right for you in the present moment and as you move forward.

PRACTICING GRATITUDE FOR WHAT YOU HAVE

Something else that you can dive into when you go inward is the idea of gratitude. Being thankful for what you have brings your awareness to what exists now. So as you reflect inwardly to find your truth, you can ask yourself some important questions about what really fills your heart right now. What are the things that make you very grateful? It doesn't have to be anything significant, but there is always something to be thankful for. By finding even the smallest thing to latch onto, you'll come into your heart center energy and raise your vibration.

So if you've had a stressful week at work, you could just need to take a few minutes on the weekend to regroup by journaling about a few things that you're grateful for. Maybe it's that you get to enjoy a quiet weekend, that you have a few friends to share space with, or that you just have a cozy bed to rest your head at night. No matter how big or small the things are on your list, thinking of them will shift your energy from a lower vibration of stress, anxiety, fear, or sadness into a more positive state. Your focus will move from the external stimuli that are making you react and focus instead on the things that give you a greater sense of peace, love, and joy. Essentially, you can use gratitude practices to get you out of your head when you've been stewing about what's gone wrong or how something is bothering you.

You may do a quick gratitude practice at a moment's notice to lower your stress level, or you can develop a longer ritual that you do regularly to keep you returning to this heightened state of being. The more you practice gratitude, the more aware you'll become of the good things that are available to you in life. This is a very grounding perspective to have because you're confirming to yourself that there are things in your life that support you. For example, there may be some people or groups that give you strength, security, or even a sense of connectedness. By confirming this for yourself regularly, you can shift your perspective consistently in the future so that you feel more empowered, cared for, and much more abundant.

Brene Brown talks about this in her book, *Dare To Lead*.[3] She mentions a study done where the perspective of people who practiced gratitude and who didn't was reviewed. Those who regularly practiced some form of gratitude could embrace the good things in life when they came, rather than worrying that something else would go wrong to offset it. They became more open to the idea that life could be great without immediately thinking about the bad. The participants who didn't practice regular forms of gratitude had a harder time accepting that there could be great things happening in their lives without the other "shoe dropping" to bring things down again.[4]

Thankfulness can bring us comfort and security through knowing exactly what we already have. It leaves the mystery out of wondering, waiting, and hoping for something else. You affirm you do already have something good and that it is supporting you. So when you see one good thing in your life and feel those heart-felt emotions that go along with it, it becomes much easier to apply that to other areas of your life because you've already done it. You've felt a sense of support from your community. The feeling of love from your family already exists for you. Maybe you've already experienced the sense of joy from helping someone. If you've felt it once, you can do it again, and that is a very stabilizing thought.

Now, even if you've experienced these emotions before, how can you capitalize on the good feelings with a regular gratitude practice? Well, you can turn anything into a routine if it's important to you and you're interested in it being a regular fixture in your life. First, you need to ask yourself what would work best for you. Are you interested in incorporating this into a mindfulness practice, an end-of-day routine, or a way to wake up in the morning? Take a few moments to consider where you could anchor some gratitude into your day by attaching it to other mindful activities that you may already do. For instance, journaling before bed could be a great time to add a few minutes to list what you're grateful for that day. Perhaps the middle of the day leaves you feeling low, and you'd like a boost of energy to keep going. That could be a great time to add a gratitude practice into your lunchtime. Maybe that means you just close your eyes for a moment before you eat and visualize the people in your life that make you truly happy.

You can make the practice as short or as long as you need it to be, but the idea is to give yourself more frequent points in your life where you stop to lean into the feeling of thankfulness. It will not only uplift you in those moments and open you up to a greater sense of abundance, but just as that study showed, it can have a longer-term impact on how you view life from now on. Who doesn't want to be open to more abundance in their life? Gratitude is the way to get you there because it's just not possible to be closed off, anxious, or afraid at the same time that you're feeling thankful, happy, and supported. They are very distinct energetic vibrations. So the more you can tap into the higher-level ones, the better you'll be able to find your way back to them when you need to the most.

This is also a beautiful way to see the supportive gifts in your life that you consciously choose to keep around. If you find a deep sense of gratitude for something, chances are that thing aligns very well with how you want to feel in your life. So that's a great place to identify what you want to do more of and where your values truly lie. You can dig a little deeper and reflect inward on what emotions those things provide for you and how you may attract more of those feelings regularly through who you choose to interact with, the activities you choose, and even how you show up in your life. In this way, you can use your gratitude practice as a jumping-off point to realize the key components that would truly make a fulfilling life for you.

GRATITUDE VISUALIZATION

You can use the following visualization to guide you in tapping into your heart chakra energy and leaning into more gratitude for who and what you have in your life. Use this as a stand-alone activity, or you may choose to journal and reflect on whatever comes through for you after the visualization.

Begin by finding a comfortable place to sit and focus your attention on your heart. Imagine an emerald green glowing light right there in the center of your chest. It's glowing brightly and pulsing out with every breath you take.

Now, think of someone in your family who you are very grateful for. Picture that person in your mind's eye now, and imagine that the glowing green light is getting larger. The light is expanding out a bit more while you think of this person.

Next, think of a friend who you are grateful for. As you think of this friend, envision the green light streaming through your body now.

Think of someone in your community who is a blessing to you and your community. While you think of this person, the emerald green light from your heart center is expanding beyond your physical body and into your surroundings.

Finally, think of someone in the world who has taught you something that you are grateful for. As you think of this person and what they have taught you, the green light stretches out from you as far as the eye can see out into the distance.

You are now expanding your gratitude with love and appreciation in the world. That is opening your heart center to receive even more abundance. So you send this beautiful green energy to everyone you are grateful for as you reflect for a moment on how they are all gifts in your life.

Now that you have opened your heart to this energy of abundance, the green light fades, and you return to where you are. Your energy pulls back into your present body, but your heart chakra remains open and lit with love and thankfulness. You smile softly to yourself and breathe deeply in and out.

This visualization is an energy-based version of the loving kindness style meditation, where you send love and light further and further into the world. If you'd like to use this to not only reflect on the external people and things that make you thankful but the internal as well, then you can couple this with some reflective time on what you are grateful for about yourself. Consider the characteristics or traits that you most appreciate about yourself or that most support you. Send heart chakra energy throughout your whole being as you reflect on this and affirm that you are strong and supportive of yourself and who you truly are.

EARTH ENERGY ACTIVITIES

We've mentioned several activities already that you can use to tap into the stabilizing earth energy within you. It's important to incorporate the ones that most resonate with you into your life so that you have the best chance of maintaining those practices. If you're not sure where to start, though, and you need further suggestions on how best to integrate some simple activities into your daily life, here are some suggestions to get you started.

Mindfulness Activities:

Breathwork

Doing breathing exercises can be as simple as focusing on the in-and-out breaths. You may do some box breathing where you breathe in for five counts, hold for five counts, release for five counts, and then hold again for five counts before repeating. There are also more in-depth breathwork practices that can support you with different intentions, but simple awareness of the breath is a great place to start.

Creative Mindfulness

Whether you do some sketching in a notebook or engross yourself in a calligraphy class, there are many ways you can bring your creative energy into mindfulness. Choose a media to start. You may find that coloring, painting, sewing, or even photography interests you. Lean into whatever is calling to your heart and start there. Find some quiet moments for yourself and just allow your focus to stay on the motions of creating the artwork. Draw your attention to the brush strokes, the textures, the colors, the feel of the camera, or the sewing needles in your hands. Reflect on your feelings as you go through those motions, and allow yourself the time to work until you feel your mind, body, and spirit are in a calm and grounded state.

Listening To Music

Try taking some time to make a playlist of your favorite music, find a cozy place to relax, and then close your eyes as you listen to the sounds. Pay attention to the different instruments, the pitch of the singer's voice, the rhythm of the music, and anything else that sparks your awareness at the moment. Feel the energy of the sounds with your body and allow yourself to focus solely on how the music speaks to you.

Mindful Eating

The next time you're going to plan, cook, and sit down to a meal, do so with more focus on what you're actually doing. Breathe in the scents of the foods and carefully prepare the ingredients as you pause on each one to consider what it is and how it belongs in your dish. Then eat, intending to savor each bite and feeling how your body responds to what you've eaten and how you receive any sensations of fullness.

Body Scan

Give yourself a few minutes to sit or lie down in a comfortable position. Close your eyes and focus on each area of your body, starting from the tips of your toes and going to the crown of your head. Identify any sensations in the body and how it feels. Let go of any tightness you may feel in each area and allow your body to unwind naturally. You can imagine sending soothing white light energy to any parts of the body that may need relaxation to put you in a greater state of calm.

Momentary Awareness

During any activity you're doing, you can always bring your attention to the moment. Imagine that you are stepping outside of yourself and becoming an observer of what is happening. See the experience from a bird's-eye view as if you are documenting everything that is going on. Take in every detail as if you are chronicling it as a vivid memory for later.

Grounding Activities:
Immerse Yourself In Nature

As we've discussed, surrounding yourself with Mother Earth is an incredibly grounding practice that will get you out of your head and rooted in your connection to what exists around you. You get to decide the level of "earthing" you need and want. At the smallest level, you can choose activities such as sunbathing, gardening, listening to the birds, stepping outside to get some fresh air, or even eating lunch outside at a pleasant picnic spot. On a grander scale, you can go all out and swim in a lake, plan a hiking trip, go camping with your family, or even ski down a mountain. Most days, you could perform simple activities to ensure that you're continually staying grounded. Then on special occasions, it might be time to do some deeper grounding work to balance your root chakra and stabilize your energy.

Cooking And Baking

This is one of the easiest ways to infuse grounding energy daily. You can use each meal as an opportunity to ignite your senses and honor the sustenance the earth provides for you. Find recipes that use a variety of fresh produce, including herbs and spices, and don't be afraid to try new things that will test your taste buds in different ways. You could choose to make your favorite meals to find more comfort and support in those on the weekdays, and then incorporate some interesting recipes on the weekends or holidays to see how they connect with you.

Craft Projects

Using your hands to make something is a great way to bring some physicality into your days. Choose activities such as knitting, woodworking, jewelry-making, scrapbooking, or anything else that allows you to manipulate various materials to create something unique.

Sports And Physical Activities

When you move your physical body, you bring awareness to each movement and connect with the energy you're creating. Whether you're doing yoga, running in the mornings, or taking a dance class, you can use the time to feel how supportive your body is of the activities you're doing. It's strong enough to keep you balanced, aligned, coordinated, and active.

Centering Activities:

Journaling

Having a journaling practice can keep you connected to what's truly important to you and what makes you feel like your true self. Try giving yourself time in the mornings or evenings to jot down thoughts and feelings about the person you are right now and how you are living the values and characteristics you want to display.

Energy Visualizations

The idea of re-centering your energy is really about drawing your power back to you. So you can set the intention to do this and then close your eyes for a few moments to visualize the energy you've given away as it comes back to you. See it as a vibrant light that retracts back into your body and energizes every area, including your aura field.

Yoga And Chakra Work

Yoga is a great way to feel empowered in your mind and body. Alongside the grounding root chakra yoga poses and correspondences found at the end of this chapter, you can also focus on your solar plexus to bring you back to your center, support your sense of self, and bring you more confidence in who you are. Include yellow foods, crystals, candles, chamomile tea, or essential oils such as bergamot and lemongrass in your routines. Coupled with the root chakra work, this will stabilize you.

Your Favorite Hobbies And Pastimes

When you do activities that make you feel you're in your element, you're giving yourself the chance to bring more energy back to your mind, body, and spirit. You could do anything from reading your favorite book to spending the day going to places that make you happy. Make a list of what makes you feel like your best self, and then set aside some time to do a few things you've listed.

Activities To Go Within:

Guided Meditations

Listening to guided meditations is a great place to start when you want to clear your mind and focus on just one thing. You can do guided meditations for a variety of intentions. Choose something that resonates with what you want to focus your attention on, or perhaps even what aspects of yourself you'd like to dive deeper into.

Tarot Reading

Tarot is one example of a practice that can help you tap into your inner guidance and intuitively find the answers to your deepest questions. It gives you the chance to reflect on something and then allows your subconscious thoughts and higher awareness to interpret the meanings of the cards you draw. Try incorporating this practice into a more in-depth ritual for yourself, or just do a quick card pull when you need it the most.

Shadow Work

When you perform shadow work, you're going into your deepest thoughts and feelings to uncover what may hold you back from your highest potential. The idea is to bring the parts of ourselves we usually hide away to the surface so we can identify them, reflect on how they are serving us, and then decide whether to release or shift them into something better. Yoan do this through coaching, quiet contemplation, meditation, journaling, or any other means that allows you to consider what you may be afraid to confront.

Dream Journaling

Our dreams are places where we connect with our subconscious minds, our higher selves, and any universal energies beyond this physical reality we'd like to tap into. When you establish a practice of journaling about your dreams, you may find messages or interpretations about everyday life that reveal themselves to you. Paying attention to these messages and identifying what they mean for you can support you in understanding your path and your most authentic self.

Gratitude Practices:
Morning Thankfulness

The morning, right when you wake up, is a great time to step into your heart center and immediately acknowledge the beauty of what is present in your life. You can do this by telling yourself a few things you are grateful for and visualizing them in your mind's eye. It will set the tone for the rest of the day by putting your initial focus on the things that bring you the most support and comfort. Then you'll have an elevated sense of perspective before any other stimuli come into your awareness for the day.

Evening Wind Down

You can review all that happened each day and find at least one thing you can appreciate before bed. It may be the smallest thing, like a healthy breakfast, or maybe you had a meaningful connection with a new friend. Even just anchoring yourself with one thing from the day can give you the feeling that the day was a success and that you can rest peacefully, knowing something was supporting you that day.

BEST TIMES FOR EARTH ENERGY

You may find that you need to tap into your earth energy at different times of the year. Winter is the time that most corresponds to earth energy as it's when the earth itself goes dormant and takes a rest before any more growth occurs. So during this time, you may naturally feel like going within and doing more activities, such as cooking, craft projects, or reading and journaling. Listen to your body and intuitively lean into whatever you feel you need. It's coming into your awareness for a reason and making you mindful of what you need in order to reset.

Now, winter will not be the only time you'll find yourself in this cycle of energy. Other valuable times to perform these practices include before and after a busy week or an extensive project. When you use grounding, centering, and rejuvenating activities before starting something, you are generating fresh energy for your mind, body, and soul so that it can take on new things. After going through a major project or a really busy time, you may use this to wind down and reset so that a new cycle may begin again shortly. Basically, you can use earthy activities as a buffer zone that delineates space between the active growing seasons of your life. Without this time, there will be no rest or time to honor what has already transpired. So give yourself as much of this time as necessary before getting back out there and reaching a new level of growth.

I suggest you plan some earth activities for every day, week, month, season, and year. Depending on what lifestyle you want to create for yourself, you may choose to establish some rituals that you do regularly that connect with who you are and what you love. Those might be things like taking a walk every evening if you love being outside or maybe establishing a meditation practice every morning if you enjoy the quiet space. Then, you can add more complicated activities such as hiking or camping trips, food tours, or yoga retreats on a seasonal or yearly basis to immerse you fully in earth energy at select times. This will help balance out the constant need to get a sense of stability with an intermittent way of filling your cup as a baseline for you.

Take some time to write about which activities and times you'd most like to set aside for your specific needs. If you're feeling like you lack any time to reflect and go within right now, then maybe you'll want to start a daily journaling practice. Maybe you think a seasonal day trip would be nice to fill your cup every few months. Then pencil it into your calendar and make it a point to plan some activities that will provide exactly what you're looking for. You get to decide how to implement this, but you have to sit down and actually consider what makes sense for you. Then, make it happen by anchoring the activities to things you already know you're highly likely to do, such as eating breakfast in the morning or climbing into bed at night. Schedule your journaling time to coincide with your breakfast. Do some breathwork right before you go to bed. Doing this will not only give you a very clear reminder of when it's time to work on your new priority, but it'll also make it a more integrated part of your lifestyle and turn it into a natural part of how you live your life.

BEING OPEN TO THE BENEFITS OF EARTH ENERGY

It doesn't really matter how you choose to bring more of this earth energy into your life. The most important thing is that you implement something as much as you can. When we're in a state of constant busyness and interchange with life, it's impossible to find the peace that we truly need. Peace comes from having a calm state in your mind, body, and soul. If you're too busy worrying about the problems of the day or what's going to happen tomorrow, you won't be able to stabilize your energy enough to find peace.

Removing yourself for a while from the external noise will help you find that state of calm more easily and get to a place where you feel stable. Then you can see that it is within your power to create that all the time. So the more you go within, step into gratitude, ground and center, then the more you'll be able to flex that muscle when you actually need it amongst all the noise of the world. That is a genuine gift you can give yourself because no matter what the world tries to throw at you, you'll have the inner strength and calm to step into observation mode, consciously reflect, and tackle it more intentionally.

I've used this with my son before, as he can go into a state where the surrounding stimuli are too much for him to handle. He becomes overloaded energetically, and can get stressed to where he physically needs to release the emotional energy he's taken on. There have been many days after loud school events, doctor's visits, or even kid's parties where I've had to take him aside to do some box breathing or visualization exercises. These practices have not only brought him comfort, but they've also helped me to know that I am supported with tools as the caregiver. As a result, we would both come out of the experience feeling more at peace with the situation and our ability to handle it.

Besides the feeling of more stability and strength in yourself, these earth energy practices will also open you up to a lot more clarity as you continue moving forward in your life. If you never make the space for new insights and awareness, your mind will be too cluttered to show you new ways of doing things, new opportunities, or even the things that serve you best. Make space by retreating for a while and coming back to yourself. Be willing to see when life is crowding you; you need to separate yourself from everything piling up. It's through this separation that the clarity will come through. When you're immersed in cooking a beautiful meal or deep into your mindful movement practice, that is when you'll receive those "aha moments" that shift your perspective and bring you to the next level. You need these practices to make those moments happen more regularly.

Earth energy is a powerful tool in your overall life fulfillment because it will always bring you back to the moment and the joy that exists now. To create fulfillment, we must stop constantly searching for the next thing or striving to achieve more. Finding happiness where you already are will bring the greatest fulfillment to you and allow you to enjoy your journey one step at a time. When this happens, you will live life from a state of satisfaction and wholeness rather than longing and lacking. Each moment becomes respected and cherished. Each day becomes beautiful in its own way, and you worry much less about falling behind or needing to be somewhere further along.

Meik Wiking, CEO of the Happiness Research Institute, suggests that tapping into your senses and getting fully present will allow you to have deeper memories to be connected to throughout your life. He says, "The more of your senses–sight, smell, hearing, taste, touch–you can use, the more vividly you can remember, and the more cues you line up, the more likely it is that you can hold on to that memory and retrieve it."[5] Life becomes a richer experience for us to reflect on when we take the time to get present in the moments and fully immerse ourselves in them. Then, we can take those memories with us and draw upon them later to recall the emotions and fulfillment we've already experienced. By doing this, we can pinpoint more fully the abundance regularly present in our lives and the full extent of what is available to us along our journey.

Thus, earth energy, in its simplest form, is about you and your deepest connections in each moment. It's your connection to the earth and the universe. Within that, we include your connection to yourself through your thoughts, feelings, and emotions. And it's also your connection to honoring what you need so that you may restore your energy and rejuvenate your mind, body, and soul. Beyond that, at the most profound level, earth energy can bring you your greatest strength, reach into your soul to deliver your inner truths, and pull you back from the edge of frustration into a healthier way of approaching life.

Use your earth energy wisely and cultivate it like a garden that will grow abundantly if you choose to water and care for it. As you move into the next energy cycles, you'll find that this time of restorative mindfulness sets the tone for how you show up in the rest of your life, and determines whether you shrink from life's journey or hold your inner strength to move through it with more grace and peace.

EARTH AFFIRMATIONS AND CORRESPONDENCES

In order to make this section more applicable in your life, you can use the following affirmations and correspondences to integrate the pieces you want and need into a more cohesive daily routine.

Chakra: Root

Moon Phase: Waning Moon

Intentions: Strength, stability, safety, financial security, health and physical wellness, grounding, centering

Colors: Red, black, and deep brown

Crystals: Red jasper, ruby, garnet, black tourmaline, obsidian, hematite, smokey quartz

Foods: Red berries, red peppers, tomato, watermelon, meat, earthy spices such as cinnamon and nutmeg

Scents: Cedarwood, sandalwood, vetiver, cinnamon, patchouli

Yoga poses: Chair pose, bridge pose, mountain pose, warrior pose, downward dog pose, bound ankle pose, squat pose

Affirmations:

I am safe and secure.

I am fully supported in who I am and in the decisions that I make.

I am healthy and well in my mind, body, and spirit.

I am financially secure and abundant.

I am resilient and strong and can get through anything.

I am content with where I am and who I am in the present moment.

I feel protected at all times.

I am supported by the earth and all of nature.

I love and accept my body exactly as it is.

I am thankful for all that I have at this moment.

I have everything that I need.

I feel centered and deeply rooted to my authentic self.

I have people around me who support me no matter what.

My body supports my daily life.

I feel safe and comfortable in my home and in all of my surroundings.

CONTEMPLATIVE MEDITATION

Give yourself some quiet moments to reflect on how grounded you are currently. Consider what aspect of earth energy is most lacking for you right now and focus on the following question:

Where does my attention need to be directed in order to feel more balance in my earth energy?

Close your eyes and repeat this question in your mind. Place your palms facing upward on your knees, allowing yourself to become open to any insight that may arise. Imagine the thoughts weighing you down and the stress within your body slowly melting from the crown of your head to the bottoms of your feet. Visualize it seeping into the earth below you so that it may lighten your energy and enable you to feel more available and open.

Repeat the question back to yourself here and pay attention to the first thoughts or feelings that come to you. Observe them without judgment and thank your inner guidance for these insights. Bring your focus to your breath as you breathe in and out. When you're ready, open your eyes.

You can jot down any insights that came to you during this contemplative meditation in a journal, or you can record them as a voice memo to yourself for reference.

When you're ready to incorporate some earth energy cycles into your lifestyle, start by returning to this exercise and the guidance you receive from it. This is the best place to start so that you're intuitively leaning into what you need to balance first.

1. Decide on 3-4 core activities that keep you feeling strong, supported, and grounded. Make space in your calendar to do these consistently each day or week.

2. Make a list of 5-10 activities you're interested in trying out or would like to schedule into your calendar as bigger activities to focus your attention on grounding, centering, and going within. Create a plan for how you'll incorporate these into the next 6-12 months.

3. Set aside a time to do the grounding visualization and the contemplative meditation in this chapter. Be sure to take a few moments afterward to journal any insights that came to you during the exercises.

4. Take a few moments each day to focus on your breath. Breathe in for five counts, hold for five counts, and then breathe out for five counts. Give your full awareness to your body and any physical sensations you have at the moment.

1. Bernstein, Gabby. (2016). The Universe Has Your Back: Transform Fear To Faith. Carlsbad, CA: Hay House, Inc.
2. Dispenza, Joe. (2017). Becoming Supernatural: How Common People Are Doing The Uncommon. Carlsbad, CA: Hay House, Inc.
3. Brown, Brene. (2018). Dare to Lead: Brave Work. Tough Conversations. Whole Hearts. New York: Random House.
4. Brown, Brene. (2018). Dare to Lead: Brave Work. Tough Conversations. Whole Hearts. New York: Random House.
5. Wiking, Meik. (2019). The Art of Making Memories: How to Create and Remember Happy Moments. New York: William Morrow.

The strength of the trees, the rocks, and the mountains all reside within you. Root yourself in this knowing and grow with unwavering stability.

Being Free

The fresh air rises with spring
And we reinvigorate our spirits and sing the praises of a new day
For it is time to once again take up the call of the future

And bend our minds to envision what may be
To enliven our thoughts with expressions of the past transformed into future hope
So that we may see a fresh path ahead

To rise from the hidden dark of our inner worlds
Once again, to free the heaviness that has weighed upon us
In order to bring a lightness to what we must now foresee

aligning air

Chapter Three

Air Energy

After you've had a season of earth energy where you've been able to retreat from the world and have some contemplation time to hear your inner guidance, it's time to figure out the way ahead. You're primed to open yourself up a bit and start dreaming of what could happen in the next cycles of growth. With those dreams, you've already got a solid foundation from your earth energy work, so you know more of what feels right for you and how your own inner guidance is steering you along your path. Now it's time to take that foundation and turn it into a plan for how you're going to shape your life from this point forward.

This is where you step into the energy of the air element. Embodying this energy is all about wisdom, knowledge, understanding, truth, communication, and connection. You're essentially opening yourself up to more wisdom than just what lies within to create your best path forward. So this is a time to cultivate your knowledge and understanding of yourself, your life, and your surroundings. It is crucial to acknowledge your past, present, future, and how they are connected to gain awareness and clarity of the path in front of you. As you look at your past, you'll see the experiences that have led you to where you are now and the lessons guiding you to your next level of growth.

This is also a time to be conscious of what in your life needs to be refreshed. Air represents the season of spring, so think about what happens in the springtime. Flowers start blooming. Plants and trees sprout and grow again. Animals come out of hibernation and even multiply. New life arises after the season of rest. So this is a time for all of nature, including you, to reset for new transformations to occur. You want to look at your life from this standpoint as well. Where do you need a refresh? Some areas may feel stale and need to be cleared out or shifted. Now is the time to understand yourself and what is happening in your life in order to make these shifts and clear out the clutter before serious growth begins.

You'll also want to focus on communication and connection during this cycle. You've already established a sense of gratitude for what is supporting you, so you can take it one step farther now to solidify that support with continuous connection. This is the best way to cultivate lasting relationships that will maintain that sense of support and show you you are part of something larger than yourself. We'll discuss all the ways you can feel a greater sense of connection later in this chapter, but just be aware that connection and communication will take your awareness to the next level.

So as you put these pieces of the air element together for yourself, you'll see and feel a lighter, more refreshing approach to life. The heaviness of things will clear away, and you'll have much more clarity and focus. That is the goal with this energetic cycle. We must strip away everything that is irrelevant to us and direct our attention to our truth. From this point forward, that will be the guiding light that will direct our path, and with that comes incredible freedom, oneness, and peace. That's what I want for you as you align your energy toward a more enlightened way of being.

ENLIGHTENMENT FOR YOUR JOURNEY

To cultivate knowledge about your life's journey, you'll first need to go deeper into your experiences and see what knowledge you've gained and which lessons you've learned. There is an old saying that everyone is a teacher and a student. I believe this to be true in every aspect of our lives, from the situations we find ourselves in, to the person we meet during a chance encounter. Energy shifts to allow us experiences that will shape our growth. You probably won't realize it, but a person you meet could end up becoming your greatest teacher. You could show up at the right time to deliver a pertinent message to someone who needs it. Maybe one of your greatest struggles could become the best thing that ever happened to you. We don't realize these things in the moment. It's when we look back to see what has transpired and search within our minds for how it affected us long term that we truly understand the extent of the lessons we've learned.

Therefore, it's important to look to the past from time to time in order to find the underlying lessons that have shaped us. We don't want to dwell there and constantly go over things to see what might have been. Instead, we want to observe what occurred and how it transformed us, gathering as much insight as we can about the impact of each experience. Only through this archeological process of digging can we uncover the gems we take with us now into a new level of growth. So we must be persistent in this process and not shy away from the hard stuff. That is where the best truths lie and where we can learn the most about ourselves in order to move forward.

Jeff Goins wrote in his book, *The Art of Work*, about how experiences allow us to become the person we're meant to be. He mentions that at each point where we experience something new or take action, we learn more about ourselves and the purpose we have in life."[1] If you pay attention to your life and the lessons it can teach you, you won't feel so lost. Your story will seem less like a series of disjointed events and more like a beautifully complex narrative unfolding before you. You will understand each setback, inconvenience, and frustration as something more than what it appears to be. And perhaps, as you listen to it, your life will speak."[2] It's not going to be all perfectly planned out, but when we look back and see all of the steps we've taken, Goins says that it's as if we've built a bridge from where we were to the person we're supposed to be.[3]

That is the power of looking to the past to find wisdom and awareness. The problem is that most people look at their past from a standpoint of regret, grief, or disapproval. We want to elevate ourselves to a higher way of viewing things and take responsibility for seeing what can actually help us rather than what we feel is lacking or dissatisfying. So when you look at your past to evaluate how it actually shaped you, start first from a place of self-responsibility and acceptance. By this, I mean looking at the decisions and actions you made as the best things you knew how to do at that moment. See the situations from an observer's perspective and play them back in your mind as though you're narrating a story without the added emotions you've attached to them. Look for the moments that stand out, the ones you can now relate to other decisions or actions you've taken. Basically, take your past for what it was, an experience that set you on a path and led to where you are. Now that you're here, you can choose to redefine or recommit to those lessons and reshape or solidify those mindsets that resulted from the past. You now get to decide from a place of higher awareness and personal understanding.

By appreciating past situations and experiences in this way, we're generating a more refined understanding of ourselves, our place in the world, and how we individually and uniquely see things to create the reality we actually want for ourselves. So by taking time to journal, meditate, or just think through your past, you're recognizing another one of those stepping stones that is enabling you to build a bridge to a greater version of yourself. We are growth-oriented beings, and when we're stuck in one place in our lives, we're not really living. We live to grow and grow to live. If you find yourself in a position where growth is not happening, looking at your past progression and the lessons you've gathered from it could push you out of the rut you're in and into opening up to life again.

Now, we're talking about the idea of looking at the past in order to improve our future here. In our minds, the past, present, and future are distinct because that is how we experience them. However, the present moment is all that ever really exists, and our past and future converge within it to be one within us. So when you identify the pieces of the self that you were, who you are now, and who you want to be, then you can realize that it is all actually within you now. They are all the same. You are the person who in the past may have had feelings of shyness, fear, contentment, or being carefree. Perhaps now you are the person who feels stable, supported, and focused. Then, maybe the person you want to become is abundant, deeply connected, and a confident leader.

Recognize that all of those traits of who you were, who you are, and who you want to be merge within you. You are a multi-dimensional being with the capacity to shift and transform into the person you want to be. You have a choice in how you think, feel, and act based on your present awareness and understanding of yourself and the world around you. So your energy interconnects your past, present, and future self. Yet, only you can choose how the next moments will proceed based on your ability to see beyond your limitations and move into more alignment with your truest self. Those are the traits and characteristics you must embody based on the awareness you gain about yourself and the path that's right for you. Each moment is a new opportunity to increase that awareness and see yourself in the most elevated form available to you.

So let me get you started in this pursuit. When you're ready to take some time to look at your past, ensure that you have removed all other distractions. Give yourself some grace for a moment, and remember that you can only ever decide or take action from the awareness that you have in that moment. So tell yourself that you respect the actions you've taken in the past based on the person you were. Step into the perspective of an observer only seeking to be aware of the truth in each experience, and allow yourself to uncover anything that comes into your awareness from the past. Then, choose one aspect of your life you want to look at and return to your earliest memories of that thing first. Identify what people, places, or things may have influenced you. Replay the memory as if it's a movie and see if you can identify the key points where something pushed a button for you, sparked an idea or concept, or maybe when you may have felt a deep emotion.

As you go back through your experiences, note the parts that have stuck with you the most and how they may have affected you in other instances of your life. Maybe you have carried them with you or subconsciously been living your life because of what you've learned or experienced. Pinpoint as much as you can to give clarity to the person who you are now and how you've gone through your journey. From here, you can ask yourself important questions about whether the lessons you learned, values you took on, or mindsets you created were things you'd like to continue shaping your life around. If the answer is anything other than "yes," then it's time to work on clearing some of those things up because they're most likely causing you to stay stuck rather than fully live.

DECLUTTER YOUR LIFE

Next comes decluttering. I'm not talking about just your home, although that can also be an important step here. What I'm really getting at when I mention decluttering your life is all the other "stuff" that prevents you from achieving your highest potential. So maybe that is a cluttered home or workspace for you. A lot more likely, though, is that it includes things like your beliefs, fears, relationships, prioritization of yourself over other expectations, habits and routines, or even the work or activities you've taken on in your schedule. All of this is playing a part in how you feel and the satisfaction level that you have every single day.

So it's now up to you to sort through it all and decide what needs to go or perhaps what needs to shift or to stay. You know how when you're clearing out the clutter in your home, it's a good idea to sort things based on what you will keep, donate, sell, or throw away. Well, the same is pretty much true with most things in your life. Set aside some time once in a while to sort through everything and decide what makes sense to keep or not. Piling on unnecessary things can contribute to heaviness in your life. Yet, when you only keep what fills you up and makes you feel genuinely happy, you can create the space to enjoy life and each thing you choose to keep.

So we talked about this a bit in the earth energy cycle, where you can go within and create space away from all the surrounding noise. With air energy, you're not just removing the noise, but you're intentionally stripping things away so that you're left with less overall. It's a purging process rather than just a separation, and it's meant to allow you to shed what no longer serves you energetically. From this process, new wisdom emerges, and you're left with a better understanding of what truly makes you happy and fulfilled.

Since there's energy to everything in life, including our things, thoughts and intentions, actions, environments, connections between people, and even the places we live, we take on a bit of everything we allow into our lives. It all leaves an imprint on us somehow, and with some things, it can be a significant energetic drain. Think about this in terms of how you feel when you walk into a super cluttered space. Maybe you can sense the overwhelming nature of that space just by physically stepping into it. It may feel like it closes in on you, and there's no room to breathe.

Sometimes our lives can feel this way as well. Maybe not to the same extent all the time, but if we leave things for too long, it can feel like we can barely breathe. That's a sure sign that there's too much energy consuming you and taking over the space you need to feel free and mentally, emotionally, or spiritually available to new possibilities. When you feel the slightest hint of this, then it's time to hit the pause button and see what needs to go. Come back to the knowledge you have about yourself and intuitively use it to weed out what doesn't deserve your energy and attention any longer.

Too often these days, we curate our social media feeds and what others see of our lives. Still, very little time actually gets spent curating a life that feels aligned and meaningful to us. It's time to put the focus back where it belongs: consciously selecting what's important to us on a soul level rather than just what would look good from the outside. Bring your awareness to what feels cluttered and burdensome to you personally, not how it may appear to other people. Choose your mindset, your space, and even who you surround yourself with based on the emotions they give you.

It may be painful to go through some of these things and recognize what you've been holding onto, but it's a necessary part of your growth process. Ken Wilber, the awareness expert who has merged Eastern and Western thought in his processes, states that, "The movement of descent and discovery begins at the moment you consciously become dissatisfied with life. Contrary to most professional opinion, this gnawing dissatisfaction with life is not a sign of... a character disorder. For concealed within this basic unhappiness with life and existence is the embryo of a growing intelligence, a special intelligence usually buried under the immense weight of social shams. A person who is beginning to sense the suffering of life is, at the same time, beginning to awaken to deeper realities, truer realities. For suffering smashes to pieces the complacency of our normal fictions about reality, and forces us to become alive in a special sense– to see carefully, to feel deeply, to tour ourselves and our worlds in ways we have heretofore avoided."[4] When you find something in your life that no longer sits well with you, take this as a sign that you are opening up your awareness to the truths of your soul. You're breaking down the barriers that have kept you from being your most authentic self and are allowing yourself to poke a hole in what previously kept you confined.

As you go through this decluttering process, only invite things to remain in your life that you truly love, desire, connect with, or find inspiration from. Everything else is just filler, and it's holding you back from saving that space for something that actually matters to you. Of course, this is not a straightforward process to go through. The suffering that Wilbur discusses as you identify what's been clouding your view of the world may rear up and make you feel the pain of letting go, but doing this will lift your spirit and raise your vibration exponentially. You'll be releasing all of those heavy, lower vibrational emotions that go along with the filler stuff. Just give yourself some time to start small and address whatever is top of mind for you first. If that's your living space, set aside a couple of weeks to work on that. If a belief is impeding your goal, find a coach to work through it with you for a month. Start where you are and don't take on everything all at once. Everything you clear will shift some weight, but it's best to ease into the process with a specific intention to see through each time you do this.

Do a review of your life, see which aspects are the most pressing to shift, and put those at the top of the priority list. A life audit is a type of review that will allow you to take a bird's-eye view of everything going on and pinpoint exactly where the problems may exist. You'll see some pieces glaringly displaying a lack of alignment or feeling very depleted. In other areas, you'll find that things are going better than ever. This is where you'll be able to make sense of what has been the most off balance and how you may sort through things to get back on track toward a happier way of being.

Limiting beliefs will be the hardest to let go of, and it's most likely that physical clutter will be the easiest. Although, no matter if it's something you've purchased and kept around or a belief you've held for a while, you're going to have to come to terms with the reasoning behind why it's there and why you must let it go. In either instance, the resulting decision should feel aligned to who you know yourself to be in the present moment and who you want to be in the future. If something makes little sense in that context, it likely needs to go into the "release" pile of your decluttering journey. Acknowledging that fact alone should bring you a great deal of awareness and freedom to step into a better version of yourself.

Before you release anything, though, it's always a good idea to appreciate what it has given you or how it has allowed you to feel, especially with any beliefs you may have had. By doing this, you are respecting the past and how it has been for a reason. It has served you until this point in your journey by teaching you a lesson, nurturing you somehow, or giving you what you thought you needed. When you can open your heart enough and find gratitude for what existed, you'll be in a better position to release it with love for it and yourself as you move on.

In the popular Marie Kondo home organizational method, she recommends practicing gratitude for everything you get rid of in the decluttering process.[5] Kondo says that, "It is not our memories but the person we have become because of those past experiences that we should treasure."[6] We can apply this to keepsakes in our homes and the mindsets that we've held. They have all played a part in shaping who we have become. As you find the role that each played, acknowledge it, and show gratitude, and then intentionally choose to create space for a new way of being that is respectful of the person you want to become. Ultimately, this is synonymous with the person you know you already are but have yet to match the current physical reality with. Through this purging process, you can systematically reconnect that better version of yourself to your physical realities so that they finally match.

DOING A LIFE AUDIT

Years back, I had a pivotal moment that allowed me to take stock of where I was in my career and in my life as a whole. I remember standing outside in an open dirt field, watching a few people around me scrambling on their radios to coordinate the clean-up of a major incident that had happened shortly before. My boss had just arrived on the scene, and as I stepped back to watch him take over, I could almost feel the separation between me and this place. It was as if time was slowing down for those few seconds so that I could really see what it would look like as a part of this "world." I saw who I would have to become if I stayed in the military. The path played out in my mind's eye, filled with missions that weren't really mine and deployments that proclaimed to be for a higher good, but that were usually just lip service to cover up some underlying agenda. I saw the long hours working to create something meaningful, only to have others determine we wouldn't see the project through. Most of all, I saw a journey that would take me to a place I no longer wanted to be, and in that moment, I knew I had to make some changes.

There's no doubt in my mind now that before this moment, I had gotten signs that my path needed some adjustments. I had struggled and pushed myself hard onto the path of being a military officer. It was what I thought I wanted: to become an accomplished, well-respected leader who could make a difference. I did enjoy my military job as a project manager, and it felt fulfilling to see something I had worked on come to fruition. Yet, it never really clicked, and I always felt that it was just off somehow. No matter how much I enjoyed watching a new building go up or reviving a thirty-year-old one to new standards, it still wasn't fueling me toward somewhere I wanted to end up eventually. So I slowly reevaluated the direction of my life, and in that moment, standing in the open dirt field, I knew the reality of the path that I was on just wasn't the path that I expected it to be, nor one that I cared to keep walking.

From there, I had to take a long, hard look at what I had been doing. So I realized I had been pushing to make things work for way too long. I needed to pull my head up, stop looking down to check all the boxes, and take a higher bird's-eye view to see what was really available to me. I now had my eyes wide open, and I was ready to see further out into the distance. Once I opened myself up, it became pretty clear that what I had been working so hard for, while giving me lessons and experiences that I was incredibly grateful for, just wasn't aligning with the person I wanted to be or who I saw myself as from that point forward. So I had a choice to make. I could keep going and lean into those "sunk costs" as financial experts call it when you've already invested so much into something without seeing the results you want. Otherwise, I could find the takeaways from that experience and move into a new direction that felt more connected with the future self I was interested in becoming. Thankfully, when the opportunity presented itself to me, I chose the latter. I was open enough at that point to see that I needed a new direction, and I took a chance to separate from the military and recommit to finding a path I actually wanted for my future.

Jeff Goins, says, "Chances come to us all, but only those who are ready recognize them. You don't need some big plan. You just need to be a little dissatisfied. You need to have some vague premonition that the world is not completely right. That's what awareness is: a sense that something more is possible."[7] While Goins is talking primarily about your calling in life, it's applicable advice to anything that needs to shift for you. Your job, your relationships, your health, or any other part of your life all require a sense of awareness around whether they make sense on a deeper level for you. Why invest time and energy into them if they have no meaning? You must be aware of what is working and what isn't to make a change when the chance comes along. Be ready and willing enough to respond in a way that puts you in the driver's seat of your own life.

Hopefully, as you step into more of your own air energy, you'll be able to practice doing this a lot more and come to a deeper understanding of who you are and what opportunities could be truly beneficial to your soul-centered growth. Find the time to take the bird's-eye view and just have a look at where you're headed. I'm sure you've probably heard the expression of missing the forest for the trees. Don't be the person who misses the forest of their own life. Step back from time to time and assess. Permit yourself to question everything around you and all that you're doing. Look at everything in relation to each other and see if it all makes sense in the greater context of your life.

To do this very deliberately, you can create a life audit for yourself. Take some time to become an observer of all that you see happening. Evaluate each aspect of your life from your career, family, and relationships down to your spiritual and personal growth. Dive into the energy you feel in each area and how much it brings you joy, fulfillment, and motivation, or a lack thereof. Out of this awareness, you can make some tough decisions about what is and isn't working. Just remember to be gentle with yourself in this process. It may open up some difficult emotions, but it will allow you to create a greater depth of personal understanding and awareness around how you can make shifts in your life. Then you'll be able to open up the space you need for more fulfilling growth to occur.

So don't be afraid to look up every so often. Honor the insights that you receive about yourself and the path that you're on. You are bringing a lot to the surface as you do this. It takes great courage to lean into your inner wisdom, but it's the only way forward if you want to attain your most fulfilling life. Respect each decision you make based on your new insights, as this will be a process of continually uncovering and shifting to get to where you want to be eventually. But with every new piece of awareness you find and every part of your life that becomes clearer, you can celebrate the fact that you will be lighter and truer to yourself because of this process.

SETTING CLEAR BOUNDARIES

Along with creating awareness and releasing the things that no longer fit into the life that you want, you must also delineate clear boundaries so things don't creep back in.

This may be to decide what you will say "yes" or "no" to when people request your time and attention, or it could be for things like how you will know what to spend money on or bring home. Setting boundaries is a way for you to better honor yourself and balance your heart chakra energy because it's not always about doing things to make other people happy. You've got to have self-compassion and care enough about yourself to live the fullest life possible. When you do this, you lift not only your own energy but also the energy of everything and everyone around you.

Think of ways that you can be more fully respectful of your own truth rather than the obligations and judgments of other people, which you can't control as they are outside of you. Your truth, however, includes your beliefs, values, priorities, and needs. The intention here is to bring those things more into perspective as you determine where your boundaries lie so that you are drawing the line between what you are accepting into your life and what you are not. This is the time to take responsibility for what you consciously choose and control in your life and how you will implement this.

As you set these boundaries, you'll feel more serious about living a life in alignment with your truth. Other people and the universe will energetically feel you're serious as well. People in your life will show more respect for your clear decision-making and start shifting the way they interact with you based on your boundaries. The universe will adjust and support your aligned state with things that complement your new decisions and boundaries. This may be rough at first, but you'll be setting a new paradigm for your life, and the direction you take will become much more connected to who you want to be.

UNDERSTANDING YOURSELF AND DEVELOPING A GROWTH PLAN

Whether you're going through serious reflection times in your life when you're really questioning the big things or just walking through daily life to move forward, it's important to be aware of yourself. Knowing who you are on a soul level will allow you to feel more whole and consistently empowered to shape life how you want it to go. So building cycles of air energy into your life could be a great time to dive deeper into the things that make you feel most like yourself and bring you the greatest amount of alignment. This is where we converge mind and heart in order to place you in a position of complete clarity for each step you'd like to take from now on.

You can start first by looking at your personal character and the identities that you most naturally connect with rather than those assigned throughout your life. Do you feel very drawn to being an artist or a creator? Are you a nurturing mother and naturally take care of others? Do you have an openness in your mind and heart and feel called as a spiritual seeker? How do you see these traits coming through, or how are you exemplifying these in your life right now? Highlight some aspects of yourself that feel very connected to you on a soul level. You can look for clues in different aspects of your life to show you where you thrive and what brings out the best in you.

Then, once you've gotten a greater understanding of what makes you the soul you truly are, it's time to use this knowledge to develop a roadmap for yourself. This could be anything from developing a daily plan for routines and rituals that support you in feeling most aligned to this heart-centered self to developing a full life plan detailing all your aligned goals and what you will do to achieve them. Basically, this is where you're taking what you've found in your heart about yourself and melding it into a realistic plan using your logical mind so that you can start making it a reality.

As you put your heart and mind to work together, things stop becoming just about checking the boxes or doing what other people expect, and instead allow you to turn your inner awareness into an outward manifestation of your truest self. This way, you won't ever find yourself at a point in your life where you question how you even got to that place, as I was in those moments in the dirt field. You won't be using someone else's roadmap for life and going through the motions, putting one foot in front of the other. Instead, you'll be feeding off of your own personal truths and creating your next steps based on what will make you feel most fulfilled every step of the way.

So you have to determine what your intention is when you tap into your air energy. Do you want to plan your daily life and feel better about how you spend your time? Do you want to create a long-term vision and plan ten years out for a future that feels full and inspiring? Are you trying to develop regular practices for self-awareness so that you can create more aligned goals? Whenever you feel like planning your next steps would be appropriate, turn to your air energy and seek wisdom within. You get to decide how to use these cycles of clarity to bring your heart together with your practical mind.

I suggest starting with a long-term vision and then working backwards from there. If you don't have awareness around how all the pieces of your life fit together, then it'll be tough to piece it all together after you've gone in lots of different directions. If that feels like where you're at right now, it's best to first give yourself some space to make that super clear. After you've got a larger concept for your life, then you can look at planning individual goals and your daily life in order to refine it.

Since this is the starting point that I suggest, let's look at the idea of putting together your long-term vision. You always want to start with who you know yourself to be at the deepest levels. That's the work that needs to be done before any planning so that when you get to that point, it'll be easier to decide based on what would make you happy on a soul level. If you've already done that, you can now piece together a picture of a lifestyle you'd love for your future in the best way you can envision it at this point in time. Give yourself some time to sit down and look at all the different aspects of your life again. Think about what it would look like if each aspect were the best it could be in terms of how it would make you feel, not just regarding external expectations.

You're creating this vision around the person you know yourself to be and who you'd like to be in the future. As you grow, this will change and develop, but this will be your starting point. You can use this vision to bring awareness to the journey that you'd actually like to have. Come back to the knowledge you've gained about yourself: your personal values, beliefs, priorities, and needs. Lean into the characteristics you want to exemplify and also the feelings you want to feel. Then, connect those to the tangible pieces of your life, such as your job and home, and the intangible things, such as your relationships or how you carry yourself daily. Create an entire picture for yourself as if it's a mosaic, with each piece coming together to create a unique piece of art.

Michael Bernard Beckwith, a spiritual leader and teacher of his life visioning process, says, "Imagine the relief of removing your carefully crafted mass fashioned by societal forms of conditioning and instead responding to what comes into your experience directly from your Authentic Self. One of the first principles to honor in your relationship with yourself is to respect and trust your own inner voice. This form of trust is the way of the heart, the epitome of well-being."[8] This is what you should be tapping into when you create this life vision for yourself. Remove the outside world from the equation and instead focus on the insights you have received from your heart. It should be a freeing experience that allows you to fully express who you are and relay your truest self into a full picture of life. This is what you're going for to establish where you're actually interested in ending up and how you'd like to live while you're getting there.

Now, like I mentioned, this vision needs to be very fluid, because you will change. The whole point of life is to grow. After you have this roadmap to guide you, though, you have a direction and then you can create smaller, more specific plans for yourself from this in order to achieve all the things that you desire. For example, if you know you'd like to become an award-winning writer and that's part of your long-term vision, then you may decide to set aside a couple of days to create a plan to get you there. You can set very clear, specific, and measurable goals that focus on one step at a time to accomplish this. Maybe you'll plan to take a writing course first, and then decide on how many books to write in the next few years before entering a writing contest.

Air energy allows the mind to make sense of what the heart wants and feels in every way you can reasonably think through it. It's not just logical thinking through the present moment, either. It's having your inner convictions dictate your future direction, from the largest concepts to the smallest details. With this process, you can establish a significant amount of clarity for yourself so that you no longer feel you're floating through life or just seeing what happens and hoping for the best. You are creating the alignment you want, and this is where manifestation starts happening. The underlying thoughts within you work their way up to the surface, become more manipulatable as a realistic plan, and you see a practical way for it all to transpire. This is the genuine beauty of using air energy to shape your life from a place of higher insight and soul-centered connection.

MAKING MEANINGFUL CONNECTIONS

Once you have more clarity around what feels congruent with who you truly are, you can establish more meaningful connections. Air energy leans heavily into connection and communication so that you are in alignment with your truth in each aspect of your life. This may mean that you're connecting more often with the work that makes you feel purposeful, the people who inspire you or make you feel your best, the surroundings that make you feel at peace, the home that gives you a sense of comfort, or anything else that brings out the best version of you. This is the point where you express yourself through what you allow into your journey.

Through this expression, you elevate your vibration and understand you are part of something much bigger than yourself. You are connected to every aspect of life and never alone in who you are or what you are. Your energy connects to the people, places, and things you've consciously chosen, bringing a powerful perspective. That connection can show you the entire universe is always working in your favor, since you are a part of it. So as a result, you'll be more likely to show up for things in your life with a positive, opportunity-focused mindset and outlook because it's not just about a narrow view of your life any longer. It's about the interchange you have as part of a larger whole, working in tandem with the other pieces to bring about a beautiful journey and outcome for your life. It's a manifestation of your truth, not just a video game to be played daily.

So I want you to look at how you can amplify the meaningful connections in your life. First, address your relationships and see how you're showing up to relate to others. Look deeply at your close relationships to see how you interact daily, including how they may enliven or deplete your energy. Choose specific ways to improve your part of the relationship and take responsibility for consciously creating more powerful connections through spending quality time together. This could be through cultivating engaging conversations, doing activities that make you both happy, or learning new things about each other. Collaborate and partner with people on different projects. When you find that someone really gets you and what you're trying to accomplish, then you can lean into that understanding and fuel a much richer relationship around purposeful work or a common goal.

You can also set aside time to meet with those who are important to you in order to nurture those relationships regularly. Decide to prioritize your connections by scheduling a recurring Sunday brunch with a friend, date nights with your spouse, or time to read and discuss a good book with your kids. Open communication and constant engagement are an art that we must practice by constantly showing up and expressing ourselves in a heartfelt way. By establishing a consistent routine of this, you're giving the relationships in your life priority over all else that may distract you and you're choosing to cultivate a higher level of interaction. This will lessen the surface-level dealings you have and instead focus your attention on creating real meaning that fulfills you, sustains any need you have for support, and provides connection to something beyond yourself.

Wiking says in his book *The Art of Making Memories*, "There is no doubt that some of the most meaningful and memorable moments are when we connect with other people...The tiny moments which may go unnoticed or seem insignificant to others can be those moments that never leave us, those moments when the small things in life turn out to be the big things in life."[9] That's where we can leave behind the feelings of being so small and separated from everything around us and find comfort and fulfillment in a moment of oneness. Think about when you have a random laugh with someone over something that happens to you both. Perhaps you run into each other, one of you blurts out something funny, or you make a mess of something. In that moment, you're experiencing something together, perceiving things the same way, and finding a common way of making light of it. That moment brings you closer together and gives you a sense of synergy with that person. It's a way of feeling like you're not alone, but that you're having shared experiences that can really enhance the way you go through life.

These experiences may be random moments, but they come from constantly showing up to connect. You never really know when you're going to get moments such as these. So you can look for ways to be around people who bring you joy and share a similar perspective or identity in order to give you more connection points. Find people, organizations, or communities that feel supportive with their energy just like we talked about with earth energy. Usually, through communication, you can develop more of a supportive relationship and establish a bond that can, over time, turn into some very memorable moments. Having commonalities with people means you have a starting point, and from there it just takes a bit of effort to maintain those connections with engaging experiences that might lead to majorly meaningful moments.

Aside from your connections with other people, it's also important to cultivate a sense of connection with nature and the world around you. Wiking also mentions that it's not just about your relationships with other people.[10] He says, "When it comes to happy memories, the importance of connection includes more than other people. Connecting with nature, connecting with our bodies and connecting with the world are also common denominators when we examine people's happy memories."[11] Everything has energy, so all that we surround ourselves with can contribute to the energy that we feel in our lives. It's up to us to determine how we relate to that energy and what we choose to allow in.

So we talked about being physically present and aware when you step into your earth energy. Here we're going beyond that to more fully develop a sense of consciousness about your place in the world. You exist within the context of your home, your city and country, and even the natural environment around you. Have you ever actually taken the time to consider each one of these things in relation to how you connect with them? Have you considered what type of feelings your home evokes from you? Do you know where you feel most happy in your city? What about nature near you connects with your soul and makes you feel at peace? When you fully connect with your surroundings, you increase the chances you'll find fulfillment right where you are and gain many more happy memories that Wiking is talking about.

If you had a hard time answering some of those questions, though, chances are you haven't really given yourself time to appreciate how the world intertwines with you. You may need some space to think about how this aspect of life can enhance the quality of your daily experiences. Consider how much more peace and joy you would feel if you were to find the good in where you are. When you can extract the beauty out of your external reality, you can raise your awareness by seeing how everything supports you. I know this may be hard if you currently live in a place that isn't ideal, or you're surrounded by people who don't really seem to have your best interests at heart. Yet, this is when it's most important to see through the surface and pinpoint even the smallest of things that may work in alignment with the person you want to be.

The more you can find connection points, the greater your chances of consistently knowing you are not alone and that life wants to align beautifully for you. Now, without these connections in place, this concept may be beyond your grasp, and you could have a very hard time manifesting the things that you desire in your life from a viewpoint based on separation. Leaning into your air energy changes that through awareness of yourself and what you can bring out of your surroundings to enhance your own personal truth.

Beyond this, one more aspect of connection and communication can help elevate your perspective on life: the idea that you have higher guidance through your higher self, spirit guides, ancestors, source energy, or whatever else feels right for you. These energies are here to support you as you walk your path; through open communication, you can more frequently gain understanding and clarity with them by your side. Rebecca Rosen, a popular medium who teaches how we can all connect with spirit, says that, "Help is always available to us, even in our bleakest and most challenging moments, if we open our hearts to it. And when we do, we set miracles in motion."[12] You always have the ability to connect with your "team spirit" as she calls it, and it's through this connection that we become a bridge to our more enlightened selves.[13] Not only can you cultivate a deeper sense of awareness without judgment in this way, but you can find a greater sense of peace with who you authentically are on a soul level by reaching out to your spirit guides that only vibrate from a place of love.

To become more of an open channel for this type of communication, you first need to set an intention that you are ready to receive insight. Allow yourself to show up from a place free of expectation and be willing to hear whatever comes through. You can use practices such as automatic writing, meditation, tarot readings, or anything else that helps you connect and set your fears aside in favor of connection. Fear often holds us back from seeing what we know to be true. Here, our minds need to take a back seat so that our hearts can be open to higher wisdom first. Then we can process it mentally after we've taken the logic out of it to get us started.

You may find that it helps you to establish a common language with your higher guidance first so that you have a baseline of understanding. It could be anything from asking for signs such as numbers or songs to specifying what particular things mean to you. As you request greater insight using these communication methods, you may find more clarity available when these things show up in your life. Observe them and try to find the underlying messages. Use them as experiences to help you know your connections run beyond anything you can see with your eyes or sense with your physical body. You are an energetic being, and there are no boundaries to how the universe can support you.

Piecing together this aspect of air energy, sometimes you need to cultivate a deeper sense of connection to yourself, and the world around you to know life carries much more than what appears right in front of you. As you understand yourself better and feel the energy between you and your surroundings, you'll gain the potential to manifest reality. Your perception will shift to that of the world working in your favor. You'll find beauty and happiness in the smallest of places. Plus, you'll be able to take that bird's-eye view of the entire forest more often, seeing yourself in oneness with a bigger picture rather than just down at the tree level all by yourself.

LEAN INTO YOUR PERSONAL FREEDOM

The last piece of air energy that will support you in the higher awareness of who you are, yourself in the larger picture of life, and your ability to transcend the limitations of life around you is the sense of personal freedom that you hold. In order to grasp this, think about it in terms of how you experience air energy in nature for a moment. The wind blows swiftly across the plains and mountains and moves along with the tides. It is part of the whole, flowing alongside other aspects of nature, and yet it can direct its own path. As we experience it, there is a genuine sense of movement and freedom to wherever the wind goes. This is how we also want to express the air energy of our own lives.

We've already established that you want to create a sense of connection with the world around you, so it's not about detaching yourself in order to live freely, without strings. It's more a feeling that you are internally guided and sound enough in who you are and your place within the world that you can make choices aligned with those convictions without being swayed. In this regard, it's important to do the work to identify what freedom in life looks like to you based on your discoveries about yourself and your connections. Tim Ferris, the author of *The 4-Hour Work Week*, says, "$1,000,000 in the bank isn't the fantasy. The fantasy is the lifestyle of complete freedom it supposedly allows."[14] Society portrays this image of a financially free person as someone who has gained a million dollars and can do whatever they please.

In reality, though, it's most likely not that simple. Aiming for a million dollars could come with a significantly stressful business to run, people constantly requesting things from you which you may feel obligated to say "yes" to, the burden of maintaining high-end homes or material items that you take on as a result, the reduction in hours you get to spend with your family, or many things may actually restrict your personal freedom in the end.

Therefore, the idea of freedom is entirely subjective, and it's up to you to determine what definition brings you the most alignment. It may be in terms of money, but it could also be in relation to your time, creativity, health, or any other area of your life. Only you can decide at what point you'll feel a sense of deeper freedom in your life, but the difference it'll make to pinpoint it can be significant for your quality of life. For instance, it could be the difference between feeling at the whim of everything else happening around you versus being free to choose how to pivot and move forward consciously when something shifts in your life. It could mean rather than letting outside judgment and expectations dictate your path, you instead allow your inner compass to steer you. Perhaps it's about letting go of fears that hold you back and unapologetically showing up to be who you naturally are. Maybe for you, it really just comes down to flexibility in your days rather than stove piping yourself into someone else's idea of what you should do and when.

Now is the time to dispel the ideas of what society has told you freedom "should" look like and reteach yourself what feels more aligned. I suggest starting with an exercise where you ask yourself, "Wouldn't it be nice if..." You can fill in the end of that sentence with whatever would make you feel most free in your life, such as, "Wouldn't it be nice if I could take Fridays off to work on my creative interests?" Here are a few other suggestions to get you to think:

Wouldn't it be nice if I could live and work anywhere that I chose?

Wouldn't it be nice if I didn't have to worry about what other people thought of my work?

Wouldn't it be nice if I could go on leisurely walks in the middle of the day?

Wouldn't it be nice if I had a completely paid-off house?

Wouldn't it be nice if I was healthy and strong enough to play with my children and grandchildren throughout my entire life?

Wouldn't it be nice if I could spend my money on causes that I believed in?

Wouldn't it be nice if I could wake up whenever my body naturally felt ready to rise to start each day?

Wouldn't it be nice if my retirement account was fully funded by the time I turned 45?

Wouldn't it be nice if I could take several long vacations each year without worrying about work?

Wouldn't it be nice if I had a supportive community that encouraged me to do what I loved?

Of course, these are just a few examples of what's possible with personal freedom, but you can use these as a starting point to see what resonates with you and what doesn't. Give yourself time to let your mind and heart wander and write anything that comes up. You can review your thoughts from here and pinpoint the ones that stand out the most. Then, it's time to go further beneath the surface than just the tangible things. Look at each item that stood out and ask yourself why. Why would it provide you with a greater sense of freedom? Keep going one layer deeper with your questioning until you uncover an actual sense of connection with your inner self and core personal values. This is where you want to end up and see if you can almost feel the freeing sensation as you visualize or think about it. If you can get to that point, you know you've struck on something deserving enough to be implemented into your life.

Now, depending on what you choose, there could be things that require a great deal of work to implement. This usually isn't a quick implementation process, but it is worthy of bringing you an incredibly powerful result. So some things may require more mindset work, while others may require a realistic plan to put the pieces in motion. Just pick one or two things to focus on at first that seem like they could really affect your present sense of freedom, and that's where you begin. See how they fit into the life plan that you've created so that they make sense in the life you truly want to be living. Remember, the intention is for you to have a well-balanced, holistic life, so everything should work with every other piece. This is your checks-and-balance system to ensure you're aligning the parts to the whole. Then, once you've got a few ideas for your personal freedom that fit nicely within the larger context, you're all set to make a plan for how to turn them into reality.

Write the first three most basic steps you would need to accomplish in order to get you closer to achieving this sense of freedom. Keep them small and measurable, and realize that the outcome of these steps is constantly developing and getting closer to your bigger vision. You're doing this with each step, and the important part is that you're moving forward with some awareness and growth, along with taking responsibility for your life. If this is what you focus on, you will always be successful. Plus, you're also already exercising your own powerful freedom of choice as you do this because you're deciding that you know what is best for you and you're showing up to implement that. Don't ignore the freedom of choice you have at every moment. The more you take personal responsibility, the more feelings of freedom you can create in order to magnetize even more.

Let's talk about this concept for a moment in order to more fully understand how it can support you. Once you feel something, that emotional energy draws in more of the same. In order to achieve more freedom, you need to first embrace a sense of freedom where you currently are. Gabrielle Bernstein says, "Instead of obsessing about the outcome, focus on how you want to feel."[15] It's the underlying feelings that mean the most when you're trying to manifest something in your life. Remember when we talked about your past, present, and future self all being one? Well, when you feel the energetic vibration of what you're trying to attract more, you establish that vibration either from memory or from a current state of being. You can magnetize the same energy even more for your future self since you have already felt those feelings. They are already a part of you and will naturally connect more of that same energy toward you in the future.

Think about when you've already felt freedom. Perhaps it was when you took a day off from school and went out with some friends. Maybe you rode a roller coaster and felt like your most alive self. It could have been when you booked a trip on a whim or even when you told someone how you really felt about something. No matter how big or small the situation seemed, it still created the feeling of freedom within you. Because of this, you already know from your personal experience what it feels like, and you can replicate it once again as it's already within you. Your past or current self has established a connection to this emotion, and thus it's within the capacity of yourself at all points along your journey.

Knowing this, it's your job now to tap into the feelings of freedom in your life. Take it from Danielle La Porte, who says in her book *The Desire Map*, "Knowing how you actually want to feel is the most potent form of clarity that you can have."[16] That's the real intention behind air energy, establishing more clarity and awareness. With more awareness comes freedom, and vice versa. Having a sense of freedom and knowing what that means to you and how it serves you will open you up to more clarity. So take the time to recall moments of freedom and anchor into them. Go through the motions in your mind and feel it in your mind, body, and spirit. Make it as real as possible, and hold onto the sensation.

Then, think about what you're trying to create in terms of more freedom in your life. Connect the sensation of what you've already felt with this new area of your life. Anchor them together so that when you think of the past or current circumstances, you also think of the new areas you can shape. Do this repeatedly as you focus on the steps you must take to make your definition of freedom a reality, and then slowly build these pieces into your life one by one. If that means slowly leaving an hour or two early from work on Fridays or finding more long weekends to go exploring, then make it a point to connect that behavior with the emotion of freedom that it's giving you. Start generating more moments where you lean into your choice and build momentum from there. As long as the energy is present, you can grow it into the vision that you truly want to achieve in your life.

ACTIVITIES FOR AIR ENERGY

As you think about how you may bring some air qualities into your own life, here are some suggestions on how to do this. You can look through the list and see which ones really stand out to you and then adjust them to fit what feels best for you. There's no right or wrong way to do this, so play around and see what activities or routines make you feel most clear, connected, lighter, and freer. Those will be the ones you should lean into and do more of consistently.

Decluttering your home, work space, surrounding environment, or physical body

Air energy is about renewal, so whenever you feel you need to hit refresh or bring something new into your life, it's time to declutter. This can be the simplest of tasks like cleaning out a junk drawer in the kitchen, or it can mean completely clearing out all of your computer hard drives, email inboxes, and photos on your devices. It's about focusing on anything in your outer environment that has become overly crowded.

Creating renewed energy by freshening up the stale air in your space

The energy surrounding you is not just about the things in your space. You also need to consider air through the heaviness or lightness you feel and the overall sensations of the space. You can amplify your surrounding energy by using live plants and flowers, bringing in essential oils that activate the energy of nature, or you could even add sounds or colors that correspond to certain energies such as happiness, peace, calm, or even creativity.

Journaling or coaching around limiting beliefs and setting boundaries

When you have old beliefs or ideas that seem to hold you back, it's a good time to bring those to the surface and look at how you may reframe your perspective. Use journaling to consider what you know to be true to you, and from there you can guide some realizations about old beliefs out of yourself. This can also support you in setting new boundaries that better align with how you want to live your life to focus on your values and priorities.

Doing a life audit

Looking at each area of your life as it stands right now can be a great way to take inventory and raise awareness of what is going well and what isn't. Use your head and heart to be honest with yourself about your current circumstances, as this is the only way to evoke actual change. Make sure you document your measurements of each area of your life and why you make each determination so you can go back after you've made changes and see your progress.

Making a vision board

Creating a vision board for your future can be powerful in establishing a baseline for what you desire and the energy around those things that you want to bring into your life. You can create it with magazines, drawings, online boards such as Pinterest, or you could even get creative and write out your vision or make an audio dictation of the picture of the life you want. You can direct it toward short-term goals or a long-term vision. No matter how you choose to do it, the idea is to envision yourself bringing more of the energy you want into your life holistically.

Communicating with people and having hard conversations

Cultivating your relationships takes time and energy, but it can be really meaningful if you connect with other people in a heart-centered, open, and honest way. Find time to remove distractions and really be present with each other. Set intentions for how you will show up and what characteristics you'd like to embody within your relationships. Then, set aside specific times or activities that will allow you to be present with the people in your life. By doing this regularly, you will honor yourself as well as others. Since air energy relates to the heart chakra, this is a great way to balance out this energy center with self-compassion and outward compassion, both of which are necessary for alignment.

Getting to know yourself better and what has shaped you into who you are today

Reflect on who you are and your experiences. You can create a life timeline for yourself or do some photo chronicling to go through your life progression and look at all that you are, all that you've been through, and all that you've learned. Through this practice, you can honor your journey and find gratitude for everything that has brought you to this point.

Writing a letter to yourself, your higher self, or the people who are important to you

Connecting with your inner self and higher guidance can occur through writing and expressing yourself with an open heart. Set aside time to remove noise around you and convey your thoughts and emotions freely and honestly as if you're writing to a part of yourself that's providing support and guidance. Ask for insight or signs that will lead you in the right direction. Allow yourself to be vulnerable and willing to uncover all that you need to work on or that you need support with. Seal up your letter and tuck it away until you've received more insight or are ready to readdress any of your intentions after a period has passed.

Finding a platform that gives you a voice to speak your truth

When you can speak freely about what is in your heart, you're laying the foundation for true freedom. Think about ways you can do this in your own life. Maybe it's through volunteering and using your time to support what truly matters to you. It could be through buying products that support your values and allow you to "speak" through your pocketbook. Maybe you want to start a podcast about an important issue or write articles for a local paper. Choose a few ways that would allow you to advocate for what you believe in and give your values a voice.

Just choose one or two of these activities to get you started. You don't have to do everything here. There's value in just consciously choosing to bring more of this air element back into your life. So you can start with one thing and then increase it to more if you intuitively feel like this part of you is still lacking. That's the beauty of this elemental method. You can lean into whichever energy most naturally feels in or out of alignment. Remember, air energy is about awareness, so the more time you spend in your air energy, the more you'll be able to cultivate a greater sense of self and own your place in the world. Once you are content with how you're continually cultivating that awareness, you can shift your focus or establish just enough air energy routines to get you a consistently balanced state of being. That should be when you're secure in yourself, your convictions, your decisions, and your perceptions and connections with the world.

BENEFITS AND RESULTS OF AIR ENERGY

Let's solidify the importance of bringing this air energy into your life. At its core, your air element will bring you to a higher level of awareness and state at which you vibrate regularly. This may be through understanding yourself a lot better to make more meaningful decisions, or it could be through establishing clear plans for how you will live your life and implement your goals. Either way, when you know more and have more clarity, you can reduce the stress in your life. The pressures of living according to external expectations become a lot less burdensome on you, and there's more lightness as you walk through each day. You may know what it feels like when people say they have the weight of the world on their shoulders. Well, balancing your air energy is an ideal way to lighten this load and ensure that you no longer feel this energetic heaviness on your mind, body, or soul.

You'll be able to establish the personal freedom that we discussed, as you won't be beholden to outside circumstances. You will know what works for you and what doesn't. On top of those benefits, you'll understand why you hold certain beliefs, values, and priorities, and how those should shape your life. The things that make the most sense for your life vision will stand out to you, and this will all give you the personal freedom to make choices in relation to your highest self, not the self the world expects you to be. That's a significant benefit that few people can say that they've actually achieved.

Imagine how it would feel to know that you are clear about what you want your life to look and feel like. Imagine being comfortable enough to say "no" to other people if what they ask of you doesn't align with your vision. You're bringing your truth to the surface by doing this and refusing to settle for anything that doesn't align with who you know yourself to be. This may take a significant amount of introspection and time to reflect on your past, present, and future. Yet, you will be better able to balance your mind with your heart and understand which to follow, when, and why if it really comes down to it. This will all be because you've done the work to merge both into your awareness and deepen the connection between them.

Another incredible perk is that you will be so much more in tune with yourself, your surroundings, and the people in your life. Knowing you have a connection beyond just you will bring so much strength and ease into your life. It no longer becomes about just you standing alone throughout this journey. You are a piece of the whole, interconnected energetically to all that is, and life is working in your favor. You can see this as you deepen your relationships and find places in nature and in your surroundings that feed your soul. When synchronicities appear all around you and opportunities come your way, the connection to a wider version of abundance will emerge like never before.

I want you to view this as your chance to elevate your mind, body, and soul. It's the underlying work required on your life perspective in order to shift you to a higher level of being. This is necessary to manifest all that you want in life. Think of it as fully researching a destination and planning a trip so that you can make the most of your journey. As Dwight D. Eisenhower said, "In preparing for battle, I have always found that plans are useless, but planning is indispensable." It's not about having a plan that's never going to change. The important part is preparing yourself for the journey by knowing your strengths and weaknesses, your beliefs, values, and priorities, and where you would ultimately like to end up. With those pieces in mind, no matter what comes your way, you'll be able to make sound decisions that align with your truest self and still feel like they keep you centered on who you are, unwavering for anything else. This is the ultimate level of self-awareness and oneness with your highest self, and what we gradually hope to achieve here.

BEST TIMES FOR AIR ENERGY

There are some specific times when it's a good idea to lean into this air element within yourself in order to create more awareness and lightness. For one thing, the air element is associated with the season of spring. If you think about the qualities of spring, you'll most likely come up with words such as refreshing, renewal, lightness, airy, warm, or even bright and happy. It's a season where we're coming out of winter hibernation to emerge into the light again. With this emergence comes new life, hope, and foresight around what will come in the growing seasons. Thus, we are very much aligned with these qualities through our own air energy.

As a result, you can use the actual season of spring to signal your personal time to activate these qualities. Perhaps you can set aside time each spring to declutter your home or to make your plans for the rest of the year. You could decide that you want to use it as a time to get out again and connect with friends and family as the weather becomes warmer. Spring is nature's way of telling you that this refreshing cycle should come to pass in your life again. The clearing must happen before any fresh growth can manifest. This is true for the plants and flowers, just as it is true for you. So by aligning with this cycle of the year, you can ensure that you've got a season of renewal firmly planted in your schedule even if you forget at other times of the year.

Besides the literal season, you can also lean into planning for new projects or goals either at the very start of the New Year or right before you intend to take action. As we covered, the act of planning will support you in having greater awareness of your vision and your intentions from now on so that you can make better decisions. All of your plans can go out the window as circumstances happen. Still, when you take the time to prepare for the path ahead, you'll put yourself in a much stronger position of clarity when you get there. Therefore, I suggest always planning, even if you're just looking at your overall intentions and giving yourself a rough outline of how you'd like to achieve them.

That's definitely better than winging it and leaving yourself to feel a lack of confidence for whatever lies ahead.

So give yourself at least a couple of days to set some simple plans in place before any undertaking. You can decide if you'd like to implement a more detailed plan and take longer to put it together. Though, after having managed dozens of projects big and small over the years, there will always be something unexpected trying to throw you off course. Having a few days to get your mind straight before a new goal or project will always create clarity and steadfastness in you so you can continue forward with little getting sidetracked.

My next suggestion is that you take some time at the midpoint of the year to clarify your intentions and goals. As we get further and further into the months, the distractions build, and it becomes harder to stand by those goals we may have made in the New Year. That's why it's a good idea to take some time during June, July, or August to re-validate your motivation and reassess the plans for where you're headed. Do a bit of an audit at this point to see if you're on track with your goals or if your energy has waned. You may decide that you need an immediate refresh through some heart-centered activities that get you feeling light again. It could be time to scratch out some plans and rework them. The goal is to give yourself a checkpoint to evaluate your progress, growth, and energy before you get through the year feeling disappointed in any lack of alignment between where you are and where you wanted to be.

Another instance when you could use a boost of air energy to balance you out is when you feel like you need to express yourself more fully. This may come at many times and show up intuitively or as a sense of being limited or held back. Take it as a sign that you must bring your truth out into the world and balance your throat chakra energy.

It could pertain to speaking up at work more, being more clear with your children, or even becoming an advocate for a cause that you believe in. When you get a pang that something needs to come out of you and that you can no longer hold your tongue, take a breath, gather your thoughts by combining your heart and mind, and plan the best course of action to get your truth across genuinely and compassionately.

Finally, the timing for air energy comes into play when life is feeling quite heavy and weighing on you greatly. This could take the form of obligations and requests from other people or expectations and outside forces, causing stress on you mentally, emotionally, spiritually, or physically. That means it's time to look at what's causing the heavy energy and identify things that you can shed. By taking an honest look at what's affecting you energetically, you can peel back the layers until you find the cause at the core. Then, it's a matter of rooting it out and making some intentional decisions about how to fix it, shift it, or let it go. As you do this, your energy will become lighter, and you'll raise your vibrational setpoint from the awareness that you've received. That way, your daily life won't feel so burdensome anymore, and you'll feel freer to restore a sense of lightness into your life.

Now, there may be plenty of other times when you may feel the need to step into air energy. These are just a few ideas to jumpstart your thinking and allow you to implement this easily starting now. There will, however, be situations that come up where you just feel a lack in this area. It's your job to listen to your heart and allow it to guide where your energy goes. Remember, your heart chakra governs air energy and will be the center of balance for these qualities within you. Use your heart through your feelings and connections to yourself and the world around you to guide you when you need more awareness, understanding, connection, or even more freedom. You can turn any heaviness or darkness into light by returning to what you know is true in your heart. Let that set you free in all that you plan and in all the intentions within your life, and know that there's always time to bring your mind and soul together for more awareness.

AIR AFFIRMATIONS AND CORRESPONDENCES

Use the following items and affirmations to rebalance the air energy within you. Depending on your personal preferences, you may mix and match these items and use them in various ways that best suit the rituals, practices, and needs of your daily life. All the following items vibrate on the same energetic frequency, so they will correlate to each other and create an interconnected energy that you can use to support your specific intentions.

Chakra: Heart

Moon Phase: New Moon

Intentions: Communication, self-awareness, wisdom, connection, higher guidance, truth, compassion, freedom,

Colors: Green, pink, yellow

Crystals: Rose quartz, green aventurine, malachite, jade, amazonite

Foods: Spinach, mustard greens, kale, avocado, limes, celery, cucumber, broccoli, pears, kiwi

Scents: Eucalyptus, peppermint, rosemary, geranium, tea tree, clary sage

Yoga poses: Camel pose, standing backbend, upward plank, lion pose, cow pose, bridge pose

Affirmations:

I speak my truth calmly and effectively.

I use my voice to make the world a better place.

I connect with others deeply through my heart.

I engage in open, honest communication with the people around me.

I stay true to my most authentic self in all of my decisions.

I set clear boundaries that respect myself and others.

I show up to live according to my beliefs, values, and priorities.

I honor my personal knowing and respect my higher guidance.

I acknowledge my past for what it has taught me.

I appreciate my past, present, and future self.

I gather insight from the world around me and make decisions based on my own personal truth.

I have a plan for my life and know that I am always being guided.

I am connected to the universe and am one with all that is.

I am free to make choices that make me feel like my best self.

I freely enjoy my life and embrace it without limits.

I know my truth and focus my energy on aligning with it each day.

I am aware of who I am and who I want to be.

I release all that holds me back and step into my potential.

I choose to live my life with awareness and intention.

VISUALIZATION FOR AIR ENERGY

Take a few quiet moments to connect more deeply with yourself, your higher guidance, and your intentions for your life. Close your eyes and focus your attention on your heart. Imagine a beautiful emerald green light pulsing where your heart is and let that light radiate up into your throat. Visualize the green light slowly turning into a blue color and stretching out further, rising into your forehead now. It's lighting up the point in between your eyebrows and creating a bluish, purple color here.

As you feel this light at your heart center, throat, and third eye, you feel a deep sense of calming clarity. You are connected to your personal truth. Sit here and let your personal truth come to your mind. Allow any insights to arise and flow to you. Open yourself up to them and acknowledge that these truths are rising into your consciousness for a reason. You are meant to live in alignment with these personal truths.

Now, thank your inner guidance for allowing these truths to come to the surface for you. Imagine the glowing light within you coming back into your heart center and gradually reducing to a soft light. Place your hands over your heart and feel the warmth of your body. Breathe here for a moment as you take the insights you've received and open your eyes to move forward with your day. You can use this powerful visualization to connect with the wisdom that you hold within yourself. When you need to come back to what you know to be true instead of what the world has told you, just take a moment to practice this visualization and find your way.

Life Design Action Steps
Air Energy

1. Journal, meditate, or visualize your life's journey. You can do this by pinpointing certain memories from your past which have taught you lessons, helped you grow, or solidified who you are today. Think about how you may or may not want to carry these things forward into the next cycle of your life.

2. Pick one or two areas of your life that you'd like to declutter and start releasing the things that keep that area feeling stuffy, stagnant, heavy, or overwhelm-

ing. Take the time to strip away as much as possible in order to give you a lighter, refreshed feeling.

3. Do a life audit of your present self. Look at all aspects of your life and rate them according to how they feel and how close they are to being completely aligned with what you want. Write any thoughts you have so that you may return to them after making any adjustments and compare.

4. Outline some clear boundaries that you'd like to put in place for yourself. Think about each area of your life and the person you want to be, as reflected in that area. Delineate what is beyond your energetic capacity, what you're ready to say "no" to, and what just doesn't fit into your ideal lifestyle any longer. Implement each boundary one at a time as you affirm each one is now part of who you are.

5. Develop a long-term vision for who you want to be and how you will live your life. Include as many parts of your life as you can into this vision, and then establish a short-term growth plan for how you can achieve some pieces in your vision.

6. Find at least one or two communities where you can connect with people and feel understood. Look for places that feed you mentally, emotionally, spiritually, and physically, and set aside time when you will consistently show up in these communities.

7. Identify 3-5 things that would give you a sense of personal freedom. Come up with a plan to focus on the most important one first and bring you closer to this goal within the next six months to a year.

1. Goins, Jeff. (2015). The Art of Work: A Proven Path to Discovering What You Were Meant to Do. Nashville, TN: Nelson Books.
2. Goins, Jeff. (2015). The Art of Work: A Proven Path to Discovering What You Were Meant to Do. Nashville, TN: Nelson Books.
3. Goins, Jeff. (2015). The Art of Work: A Proven Path to Discovering What You Were Meant to Do. Nashville, TN: Nelson Books.
4. Wilber, Ken. (2011). No Boundary: Eastern and Western Approaches to Personal Growth. Boston, MA: Shambhala Publications, Inc.
5. Kondo, Marie. (2014). The Life-Changing Magic of Tidying Up: The Japanese Art of Decluttering And Organizing. Berkeley, CA: Ten Speed Press.
6. Kondo, Marie. (2014). The Life-Changing Magic of Tidying Up: The Japanese Art of Decluttering And Organizing. Berkeley, CA: Ten Speed Press.
7. Goins, Jeff. (2015). The Art of Work: A Proven Path to Discovering What You Were Meant to Do. Nashville, TN: Nelson Books.
8. Beckwith, Michael Bernard. (2012). Life Visioning: A Transformative Process For Activating Your Unique Gifts and Highest Potential. Boulder, CO: Sounds True, Inc.
9. Wiking, Meik. (2019). The Art of Making Memories: How to Create and Remember Happy Moments. New York: William Morrow.
10. Wiking, Meik. (2019). The Art of Making Memories: How to Create and Remember Happy Moments. New York: William Morrow.

11. Wiking, Meik. (2019). The Art of Making Memories: How to Create and Remember Happy Moments. New York: William Morrow.
12. Rosen, Rebecca. Stay Connected [Blog Homepage]. Retrieved April 2022, from https://www.rebeccarosen.com.
13. Rosen, Rebecca. Stay Connected [Blog Homepage]. Retrieved April 2022, from https://www.rebeccarosen.com.
14. Ferriss, Timothy. (2007). The 4-Hour Work Week: Escape 9-5, Live Anywhere, and Join The New Rich. New York: Harmony Books.
15. Bernstein, Gabby. (2016). The Universe Has Your Back: Transform Fear To Faith. Carlsbad, CA: Hay House, Inc.
16. LaPorte, Danielle. (2014). The Desire Map: A Guide To Creating Goals With Soul. Boulder, CO: Sounds True, Inc.

Be the wind and let your wisdom guide you in the direction you're meant to go.

The summer spark has begun
We stand in full awareness of what we're meant to do
With light shining within us and ready to emerge fully

It is the season of possibility
And we must be ready to act with the strength and will of a thousand suns
For this is the moment that calls us to our destinies

And it is not for us to kneel
When the capabilities within us sing the song of triumph,
To ready us for what we know in our hearts and minds to be the truth of who we're meant to be

Chapter Four

Fire Energy

Fully diving into your masculine energy is the next piece of the puzzle in order to bring things together in your life. This is the cycle where you really see things happening because you become more active in the world. You can begin taking a much more outward look and realizing how you are projecting yourself and engaging with the world around you to create the life you want. This will be in terms of the drive you put toward your goals and dreams and the specific steps you choose to take in order to move forward. All of this will stem from your ability to move beyond thought and shift into your own power and motivation to manifest your reality.

As we've seen in the air element cycle, thoughts and plans are important. You need them to guide you forward and create a sense of meaning behind what you do. Once you give yourself the space to do that, the need shifts to action and momentum. It can be the shift that trips up many people. Sometimes it's more comfortable to continue thinking and dreaming rather than having to do something about those dreams. It's scary to have to act without knowing exactly where we'll end up sometimes or what the outcome will be. Yet, this leap of faith in ourselves and the universe will be the one thing that truly changes the energy in our lives. Nothing will change until we move our energy where it needs to go. We need to be the ones to turn the ship's wheel and not just keep plowing straight ahead on a comfortable course. If you want to get to a new destination, then you must steer yourself there by picking your head up and maneuvering through the landscape in front of you.

One time that stands out to me most when I embraced my fire energy included saying "yes" to an opportunity at the spur of the moment. I spent a great deal of time learning photography, doing photo shoots for local friends, and even taking lots of food photography for my blog. Yet, I knew I wanted to branch out with my skills and help more creatives and entrepreneurs who struggled with their images. So I introduced myself to a friend of a friend who owned a local boutique and pitched her some photo ideas.

Before I knew it, she was asking for a marketing video to accompany a photo shoot, which was something fairly new to me. I knew at that moment that I had two choices. I could hesitate and walk away from the meeting, gathering information and more knowledge until a time when I might be ready and she may still be interested. Otherwise, I could step out of my comfort zone and just say "yes" to the opportunity that felt really exciting and expansive, even though I didn't have a plan in place to make it happen yet. I ended up saying "yes" and working with her. I knew my overall intention, including improving my photo and video skills and working with more entrepreneurs, and this decision aligned with that. So I went for it without getting too much in my head. I figured it all out as I went, even with no trace of a larger plan in place first, and I pulled off a video that I was not only proud of creating, but that she found beneficial to use for her business.

So this is how you move into the fire energy element. You take a big breath, and you prepare yourself to get out there to embrace your path. With a clear intention behind what you do and a strong intuition, you'll be able to better navigate with more awareness. Best-case scenario, though, you'll have taken the time to have an intention and a plan during the earth and air element phases. It's not a complete deal breaker if you don't have either, but knowing yourself enough to have an intention will keep you from going down the wrong path with your actions. You can see when people jump into their fire energy having no underlying intention first. They chase someone else's idea of success. Perhaps they go to school for a career their parents want. They may work nonstop just for the money society tells them they should earn. They could even jump from one thing to the next, unsure of why they're really doing any of it to begin with. The impact of propelling yourself into a fire energy phase without first setting your intentions can be detrimental to the alignment that you create in your life.

It's up to you to come into this masculine energy by first setting the groundwork for it with purpose, self-awareness, and wisdom. If you have that, then every decision you make and action you take will move you forward on your course. You'll align as you take each step, no matter how big or small the thing is. Being perfectly honest, though, even if you didn't have any clue why you were doing what you were doing, it would be a much longer, more winding road, but the universe would ultimately guide you to finding your way. The key is to listen to your higher guidance as soon as possible so that you don't have to take all of those detours or get stuck in one place for too long. You want to get your life moving as soon as you can, and you do that by finding the soul-centered intentions underneath first and putting one foot in front of the other to correspond with those intentions. It's not the absolute end of the world if you haven't been doing this, but when you finally do start, it'll completely change the control you have over your life and your ability to turn it into a real masterpiece quickly.

To do this, shift those gears, and get out of your head and into action. It's up to you to know when there's been enough time to get to know yourself and make plans and when you must get things going. Analysis paralysis is an actual thing; it can be incredibly easy to get caught up in continuously making plans. So knowing when you've got just enough ideas to get going will help you create a spark of energy with which you can ignite an entire flame. This energy is necessary to generate anything you want in life, especially for growth and learning. You must create a tiny spark before it can expand. Holding onto our comfort zones, limiting beliefs, fears and assumptions, or anything else that makes us refrain from taking action is like trying to light wet firewood. It just will not activate because something is preventing it from getting the energy it needs. It may smoke a bit and appear to be doing something, but ultimately it'll fall flat.

Fire energy needs clarity, self-awareness, and alignment in order for the sparks of motivation and confidence to kick in. When you've got all of those combined, that's when the fire can grow. So you can't allow yourself to wallow in your own headspace for too long. Give yourself the awareness that you need to find meaning in what you want to do, so the path you intend to follow makes sense for you, and then just leap. The more you do this, the more you get comfortable taking action and putting yourself out there for real growth. This is where real learning happens and where you'll find your true self. It's not in the long-term plans and vision boards you create. It's when you put yourself out there the most and become fully immersed in life.

SOLIDIFYING YOUR CORE VALUES AND BELIEFS

What good would it do you to put yourself out there without first making your own values and beliefs concrete? This is the basis of your personal power, and your masculine energy of determination and drive depends on it. Thus, now is the perfect time to solidify the core of who you are. You'll want to draw upon the wisdom you've gained in the air energy cycles based on who you are through your past, present, and future. Use what you've uncovered to create a more substantial sense of self rooted in core concepts that strengthen you. Doing this will generate an impermeable shield for your energy, almost as if you were a superhero creating an impenetrable bubble around yourself. When things come up to distract you or throw you off course from what you intend to do, they'll bounce off you easily and allow you to maintain your strength.

We're creating an inner sense of stability here that will show your personal power outwardly as you make decisions and take action. Anytime someone asks you to make a decision for your work or personal life, you can draw upon your already determined core values and beliefs for conviction in your response. They'll guide you as an inner compass that intentionally shapes the course of your life. Think of it as your North Star that you get to place in the sky. Now, you may not know exactly where that North Star is going to take you, but you know that it's in alignment with the person you truly are and want to be. You'll know that following it means you're honoring your personal power, and no one can take that away from you. It's developed through a genuine sense of self that is much more highly attuned than the typical perspective on life that is quickly swayed. So when you look to your North Star to make your decisions, you'll be lifting yourself up far beyond any lower-level vibrations and taking the path of love, bliss, and connection to guide you.

Given that these core personal values can be so powerful, how do you actually establish them for yourself? First, you pull from your wisdom to establish and activate these. Look at the things you discovered about yourself, your personality, and your experiences through your air energy phase. The core values you hold currently are most likely a combination of the things you've melded into a specific perspective on the world. You may have already gone through these to determine if you still want to hold the same perspective or change it. Whenever you evaluate these things, it's important to note that the core values you hold could have come from things you've learned or experienced. They could also be things you've always held true within your heart and that follow your soul as guiding principles. Either way, the things that you currently see as valuable or integral to life are your current core values and beliefs, and these are the things that are shaping your reality.

If you want to change your reality and shift the way you do things, you've got to ensure that these core values truly align with what's in your soul. So from here, it's a good idea to take some time and evaluate what values and beliefs are present for you now. It could be anything from the idea that hard work makes things happen to giving importance to time with close family or even giving back to others through volunteering and charity. Make a list of all the things that may be core values and beliefs for you right now, that almost feel like a "code" to live by. Once you have a list of at least ten to twenty things, it's time to look at where exactly those values came from.

Dive into the memories and experiences you uncovered in the air element and connect them with the things on your list. Can you pinpoint when you took on each mindset? If it was a value of always protecting family, was there a memory where you remember having to protect a sibling or when a relative had to solve a problem for another family member? Maybe you have a core value of personal freedom, and you may remember a time when you were constantly getting into trouble for staying out too late beyond a curfew. There are usually instances that spark values in us and instill a sense of self that's connected to certain feelings we want to cultivate. These values may have aligned at the time we created them in our minds, but they may not now. This is the time to identify this and see what needs to be transformed in order to keep only the core beliefs you truly want in the next season of life. Look at each belief here. Honor how it gave you a distinct worldview, and then turn it into a more aligned value that will serve you better.

As for the beliefs that may have always been intrinsic to you, you'll want to reaffirm these for yourself now. These may be things like the value of creative expression or the idea that everyone deserves compassion. These internal, soul-imprinted values will have steered you along your course in life from the very beginning. You won't really be able to pinpoint an exact time when you absorbed these values because they were constantly present as part of your soul's expression. So take this as an opportunity to validate those as part of your life perspective, how you show up, the energy that you emanate in the world, and the basis of how you live your purpose in this lifetime. These will be foundational in the powerful sense of self that you cultivate here.

Now, as you go through your list of values and beliefs, you'll probably refine it down to three to five very significant core values that guide absolutely everything you do in life. These will shape every interaction, every decision, and every way that you carry yourself each day. Plus, a set of secondary core values will come into play on important occasions to help steer your course. These could be things like the idea of financial freedom. Knowing that you highly value financial freedom and what that means to you exactly will give you the ability to make decisions from a place of personal power. For instance, if a certain job offer would give you the chance to save more for an early retirement, then that may be a simple decision to make if you know that financial freedom is a top priority. If your core value was instead having a lot of family time together, then that job offer may not be so appealing if it meant longer work hours that kept you at work until after your kids went to bed. Do you see what I mean about making choices easier? As we said in the air element chapter, clarity comes from getting to know yourself on a deeper level and understanding how to stick to your own personal truth no matter what happens. This is a critical aspect of being able to steer your own ship and know that you will get to where you want to go.

As you step into the fire energy that drives your masculine side, it's important to solidify a few core personal values that cultivate a sense of empowerment within you. No one else chooses for you as you move throughout your life. Only you can be aware enough to take action from a place of power and conviction, and it starts with strength in who you are at your core. This awareness can't be from what anyone else tells you to be, but only from who you know yourself to be now and as you head into your future. From there, it's just a matter of putting these core beliefs into practice in your everyday life, especially when it's time to choose and act. Start with the three to five most important values and ensure you're living your life by those daily. If you aren't doing that, then focus your attention on taking action to change that right away so you can start feeling more aligned with who you are. You'll have opportunities to incorporate the rest in the right timing. For now, you can start with building up the personal power to know exactly what those core personal values are and being prepared to implement them when you most need to take action and live them fully.

BUILDING YOUR CONFIDENCE

With a greater sense of self, you can look deeper at your confidence levels as you cultivate your personal power. Confidence is something that comes from within and expands out from us as energy. It's felt through your personal presence in the world. When you exude confidence, other people connect with that strength and power right away, and they'll intuitively understand that you do not sway easily by outside forces.

Think about when you've encountered a confident person before or maybe heard them speak or lead. Usually confident people have a stature about them, where their physical presence matches their verbal communication. They look and express themselves completely differently than someone who may be afraid, nervous, unsure, or even scattered. It's like the difference between a sunflower standing tall and shifting toward the sun versus a sagging, limp-petaled weed wilting in the sun. You can sense the difference in energy in every way. The same is true for confident people. It's possible to hear the power in their voices. You see it in the way they carry themselves. You feel it in the emotions that they convey. They are strong sunflowers standing tall and unwavering. Being a sunflower instead of the limp weed is really about personal awareness and how you've chosen to apply that in your life.

When you have inner convictions stemming from your core values and beliefs, you can develop your sense of empowerment around those and use them to affirm who you are in the world. Your personal perception of the world is the one that matters most. Everyone else will hold a different perception of life based on their own values, but yours is the one that matters in cultivating the life that you want to create. So no one else's opinions, judgments, or expectations have any meaning toward your own reality, only your viewpoint. When you understand this, you can use your personal values to stand tall with your convictions and not sway to anything outside of you. It's all superfluous to who you are and what you're trying to create: a reality aligned with your best self.

The more you think about your core values and beliefs, anchor daily life in those personal values, and make choices from a standpoint of what's important to you, the more your confidence will build. You'll present yourself in the world with clarity and conviction in order to be seen as that sunflower much more often. Plus, as you align your actions and see actual results that make you feel good, your confidence will build even more and turn into further momentum to propel you forward. Results always bolster confidence because they're tangible. That means instead of ideas just being in your head and having faith in your beliefs, now you're seeing the real fruits of your decisions manifest in real life. So you can better connect them to how they make you feel. When this happens, it can really elevate your confidence levels and put you in a better state to keep going with your goals and dreams. We want to cultivate this, but it all stems from the inner strength you must develop first by developing a strong sense of self.

TAKING SMALL, INTENTIONAL ACTION STEPS

The best way to create momentum in your life is to take small but deliberate action steps. If you've already worked on a plan for either the near or long term using your air energy, then now is the time to implement the goals that you've laid out for yourself. Each step you take is important to further your growth and development, and there's no step too small for progress. Every single action creates energy, and even the tiniest amount shifts stagnation and allows for a bit of necessary change in order to make things happen. Keeping this in mind, you can start wherever you are and take the pressure off to put too much on your plate all at once. It's not about loading yourself up with a huge to-do list, but giving yourself the ability to create incremental shifts that will eventually move mountains together.

After I had left my project management job and finished up my master's degree, all I knew was that I wanted to be my own boss and do something inspiring for my career. I was a bit out of my comfort zone with no real check boxes to follow for my career path. I did not know what my career would look like, but I knew I wanted to try different things. At first, I just got started by establishing a small at-home studio in our little British townhome where I could make wall art, personalized cards, and party supplies. My head was spinning with all the ideas of what I could do and create, but I put my head down and focused on what was right in front of me. I started designing graphics and writing poems to include in my wall art and on my cards. I put my energy into taking creative action, and through those small actions, more clarity came, as did a sense of growth and accomplishment for what I was creating. If I hadn't started with those small steps, I wouldn't have realized how central creative freedom was to my life's journey and the work that I ultimately wanted to do.

If you're struggling to start or get out of your comfort zone, start with the idea of manageable and measurable steps. The more honed in you can get with what you can do in the moment, the quicker you'll see results. When we look at what's right in front of us, we feel more capable and empowered to achieve it. It's looking at the miles and miles ahead of us that can pile on the pressure and make us feel incapable of accomplishing what we want. So break up your goals into the tiniest pieces possible that you can do within a two-week window or something similar to start. Keep your intentions simple so you'll have enough courage to jump in and take action. Lean into the easiest stuff first. Give yourself positive affirmations to anchor into your core values and who you are. Then, be open to creating that energy in a positive direction by just doing one thing to get you going. Even if it's as simple as gathering materials, putting your workout clothes out the night before, or buying a new domain name for your website, do these tangible things first. There's absolutely nothing wrong with starting with where you are, because ultimately, this will give you the energetic nudge you need to keep going.

Another good thing about just taking the first steps is that courage comes from doing, not from staying stuck in your head. There may always be a certain amount of fear lying below the surface of any new or big endeavor, but you have the power to reframe it and move past it. Keith Ellis, author and goal-setting expert, describes this fear and discomfort as a movie we play for ourselves in our minds. We tell ourselves a certain story, possibly even unconsciously, that will prevent us from changing our habits or actions because we fear the idea of this movie actually playing out.[1]

So we need to adjust this movie enough to feel comfortable about where we're headed. Ellis says, "To change your movies, think of your mind as your own private movie theater...You can show whatever movies you choose for as long as you choose. You can run the same movies over and over, or just your favorite scenes. If you don't like a movie you're showing, you can stop it mid-scene and show something else."[2] You are the one in control of your mind and what you're allowing to keep you stuck in one frame of thinking. When you get out of the same mentality that's been playing for you over and over, you can take the first step into a new story and let that courage throw the old fears out of the window.

Giving yourself the tiniest bit of a perspective shift can mean the difference between staying spinning in your head and taking that first critical step to tackle your goal. So no matter what your head has been saying to you all along, just that one small step forward can help you work up the courage you need to keep going. Who doesn't want to say they were brave enough to act when it was important? You can be the hero now for your future self by changing up that movie in your head, pushing the fear aside, and taking the first step to getting you moving. If it's calling to your soul to do something, then the chances that the underlying fear is guiding you toward your destiny is highly likely. Pay attention to it and start with the smallest action you can to jumpstart your courage and change how you view what you can do. Then, put one foot in front of the other and stay out of your head as much as possible. The confidence and courage will continue to build as you take more action.

The other thing to remember here as you move forward with your fire energy is that sometimes people tell themselves that the actions they're taking are meaningful when that may not be the case. Be aware of where your energy is going at every step. Ask yourself if you may be creating busy work to avoid any fears underneath what you really should be doing. Do your best to focus on the actions that truly move you forward, not on the ones that make you feel like you're doing something. Tim Ferriss says in his book, *The 4-Hour Workweek*, "Being busy is most often used as a guise for avoiding the few critically important but uncomfortable actions."[3] Getting uncomfortable is part of creating change, and that's what living is really all about. We've got to be constantly creating change within ourselves so we can grow. A bit of discomfort is necessary if you want to get to the next level in your life, and accepting that will make your journey much easier.

That said, it's okay to fear things while taking action. Awareness through the process is the important part that will help you slowly erode that fear and turn it into more positive thinking. As you continue to take action on your goals and plans, you can repeatedly check in with yourself to see where your energy lies. Consider your emotions, your motivation levels, and what intuitively feels aligned for you at the moment. You can also assess if your activities are bringing you actual results. When you check in with these things, you'll have a reasonable view of what's working and what's not, so you can continue forward or pivot onto a better path.

Clearly, growth is never easy, and our limiting beliefs and fears come back in different forms, no matter how many times we address them. They present themselves in different ways to ensure that we've looked at them from all angles and really harmonized the energy within ourselves that must be balanced for true growth. So give yourself some grace in this process and know that reaching your goals is a challenge. You're meant to stretch yourself and constantly evaluate if you're in alignment. The key is to honor who you know you are by following through with the hard things, even in the face of limiting beliefs and fears.

When you subconsciously leave social media up while you're supposed to be working or allow "important" phone calls to interject during your project time to push off the work that's necessary for you to do, that's when you must get real with yourself and go back to your true motivations. Think about how badly you want to achieve your goals and the intentions that lie in your heart. Expose the fears that are holding you back. Reframe them into something that supports a new, empowering mindset, and then get back to the actions that will get measurable results for you. Then show up with an amplified sense of self and the willingness to put your energy toward action with a new perspective.

Always return to your intentions and core personal values to guide you. They'll keep you aligned to actions that connect with the future self you authentically know you are. In order to track these aligned actions and delineate the progress you're creating, you may choose to keep a progress log. You can use graphs, spreadsheets, bullet journal graphics, sticky notes, or anything that you'd like. This way, you can see which days you show up to take action, which days you don't, and where your energy lies as you progress. You may also choose to use an accountability partner to talk with about what you've accomplished and keep you on track toward your goals. I've found that personal accountability usually works better than an outside source, as you know yourself. You know what you're proud of, what you intuitively feel you could do better, and where you ultimately want to be. When you find that motivation within yourself to check in, you'll create a checks-and-balance system off of your intrinsic motivation and awareness. To me, the ability to do this is much more valuable than seeking it externally. However, everyone is different and having an accountability partner can definitely be more helpful if you find you really could use an unbiased party.

That really is the hardest part about being accountable to yourself. You need to leave your judgments and expectations at the door and become an honest observer of your growth. Otherwise, it can become very difficult to not stress about where you think you "should" be or to compare yourself to some arbitrary idea of success. Purposeful alignment and any growth counts here. The result of your goals is moot, as the inner growth and fulfillment are the primary goals we're seeking here. The tangible results are just a means of achieving that growth and fulfillment.

It's easy to forget that, especially when we view things from the perspective of what is tangible in our 3D reality.

Yet, the energy and emotion underneath create our life journey and our true happiness or lack thereof. Gabby Bernstein says, "Living achievement to achievement is an addictive pattern that holds us back from truly enjoying the richness of life. When we make fun a priority and release outcomes, we can stop complaining and start attracting...The goal isn't to achieve something, but to have fun along the way to what you desire. Assuming an energy of joy is the fastest way to achieve success!"[4]

Being mindful of this will play a big role in feeling a sense of personal achievement, as it can only be truly determined by how energetically aligned you feel as you move along your path. So the best way to approach taking these small, incremental steps is really from a place of awareness about the intention and energy that lies underneath everything you do. If you can do that, your chances of creating momentum and real growth for yourself will abundantly increase.

MAINTAIN YOUR MOTIVATION

Staying the course as you work toward your goals can feel exhausting. It's best not to go full force into this fire energy all by itself because even with the best inspiration and motivation, it's still possible to overwork yourself and get burnt out. To avoid this, you can pepper the other elemental energies into your time to give you more balance and stamina to keep going. This will look different for everyone, so it's best to check in with yourself again to see what works. Perhaps you couple this fire energy with a weekend self-care routine to activate your water energy. You might choose to spend your evenings reading books on other topics of interest to feed your air energy more. Also, you could choose to go on regular hikes in nature or do some gardening to ground your energy and bring you back to center every once in a while. Combining the fire energy with the other elements is a great way to maintain your motivation and fuel you for longer cycles of growth and progress on your goals and tasks.

Look at where your motivation is coming from. Intrinsic motivation has been proven to generate better performance than with external motivation.[5] Several studies have verified that when you internally find something that drives you forward to achieve certain goals, that internal connection is much stronger than prizes, money, promotions, or anything else the world may suggest to you to get you moving.[6] This is good news for those of us who want to follow our hearts and achieve things that matter to us. Too often, people lose sight of their hearts and just set their trajectory based on the latest thing to do. Instead of being the crowd-follower, be the person that chooses to honor their own North Star. Jay Shetty, mindfulness author and previous monk, says, "To live intentionally, we must dig to the deepest why behind the want. This requires pausing to think not only about why we want something, but also who we are or need to be to get it, and whether being that person appeals to us."[7] When you consider the soul-centered motivations behind what you do, you really tap into the key to your present and long-term fulfillment. This brings you to be your best self, far more than any outside driver could.

Keeping this in mind, when you put your internal motivations front and center, they'll be the guiding light to help you maintain your actions. You could do this by posting photos of friends and family around your desk, making a travel destination the screensaver on your computer, or posting an affirmation where you can see it every day. Look at the long-term vision you have for your life and evaluate how your goals are helping you get there. Then, recommit yourself to what those goals provide regarding your emotional and energetic state. Are they giving you a sense of freedom, adventure, or inspiration? Link those things to the motivation you put in front of you every single day through pictures, vision boards, and affirmations. Then show up to honor those motivations as best you can with each decision you make.

One more thing to realize here is that it's not solely about the end point when you're taking action toward your goal. It's also about the journey. You must like the path that gets you to where you want to be. Otherwise, waiting to get something at the end would prove awfully unsatisfying every day. It may even lead to giving up altogether. For example, you don't want to choose a career like medicine just because it could provide a big paycheck and a house on the beach. If you dread having to problem solve people's ailments every day or don't enjoy working one-on-one with people, then you wouldn't appreciate waking up every day to that job. It would be miserable day in and day out, and it could be very hard to keep going. So why would you choose to go on that journey solely for an endpoint that appears valuable on the outside but doesn't actually feel good on the inside?

This same concept is true for anything you undertake. Consider how the journey connects to your soul's purpose, alongside the outcome you receive on an energetic level. We want to embrace every ounce of our lives and not only be living for "someday." We appreciate real meaning in the journey and don't want to skimp on that. Shetty relates a story about this in his book, *Think Like A Monk*, where he describes seeing the accomplishments of other monks and wanting to emulate him.[8] Yet, his teacher relates the hard work it takes to get to the same level may not be an undertaking everyone wants to repeat.[9] Be honest enough with yourself to look at your goals not only from the end perspective but also from the standpoint of how it'll feel to live them out each step of the way.

Being intentional with each action you take will ensure you continue along an aligned path. Ask yourself whether you're being driven by how you get to serve others, the inspiration you're finding, or even how you're elevating your spirituality. Press yourself with these questions to get to the root of your actions and ensure happiness for you in the everyday parts of your journey and not just in the future. Embrace what gives you joy, as this will lift your motivation and ensure you wake up each day knowing you're connected with a higher part of yourself. Find gratitude and latch onto these pieces as insights into the abundant self you claim to be now and into your future with every step you take.

SEEKING ADVENTURE

Another significant aspect of fire energy is about being active and embracing spontaneity. Now, whether you enjoy being spontaneous or if you'd rather have control over things, there usually comes a time when you need to let go for a while. It's good for the soul to just go all out sometimes, do things on a whim, enjoy the moment, and embrace life. Our lives are supposed to be lived fully without limitations. If you hold everything too tightly all the time, life will get the better of you at some point and make you look at things differently.

Being spontaneous whenever you can implies that you're choosing to say "yes" to all the beauty life holds for you, without constantly overthinking everything in your mind. When we stay in our heads for too long, we latch onto our plans and ideas too strongly and create a myopic view of how things should be happening. At some point, the soul must open up outside of the mind and be able to find its bliss without expectation. In these moments, we raise our energetic vibrations to the highest levels possible and achieve periods of pure enjoyment and connection with life. This is where we should strive to put our energy whenever we're able, as it's the one place where we can actually be our highest selves.

So, in order to do this more, you can give yourself time to go out and seek new adventures. Be open to possibilities. Expand your perspective by trying new things, and try not to get caught up in your own plans so much that you forget to enjoy all that there is to experience. Opening yourself up to adventure is a gift that will allow you to grow in more ways than you ever thought was possible. It usually comes when you least expect it, though, so you have to stay open and ready for whatever awaits you.

The best way to practice this is to set the intention for more exploration in your life. Maybe that means signing up for a cooking class, finally going on that trip to Europe with friends, or even buying a museum pass for your city. Start where you are, but be willing to expand your horizons a bit more, and always ensure that you have an open heart for whatever may come your way.

ACTIVITIES FOR FIRE ENERGY

When you're ready to activate your masculine energy and fire up your drive to get things done, you can use the following suggested activities to work on making progress. Try doing these in cycles and mixing them with other elemental activities to bring you a balance that keeps you going and maintains consistency.

Scheduling and creating systems

One of the best ways to use masculine fire energy is to create structure in your life. You can turn to your schedule to create a structured approach to your tasks and to-do list. Also, you can develop systems for how you do things regularly in your life, such as managing your finances, meal planning, taking care of your home and family, or even creating a beauty regime that you can follow regularly. Any systems and structures that you can put into place to support you in implementing the recurring tasks of life will benefit you with more simplicity and ease in the long run.

Working on projects and goals

Taking action on your goals is a primary driver of fire energy. You can create project "sprints" where you designate a certain amount of time working on key pieces of your goals with measurable results in mind. Keep a progress log and ensure that you're taking action at scheduled time frames to remain consistent and build forward momentum.

Sports and outdoor recreation

Getting out into the world and doing activities that challenge or push you to the next level can feel really rewarding. Look for things that motivate you to be a better version of yourself through training and expanding your endurance. You may also find that outdoor recreational activities such as swimming, kayaking, or rock climbing present a means for more adventure and discovery of not only the world but of yourself as well.

Connecting with friends, family, and community

Fire energy is about confidently showing up as your authentic self and expressing that into the world. Connecting with others in social settings can be a great way to activate this energy and open yourself up to living fully in a very interactional, self-affirming way. Try scheduling time with friends and family to do fun activities such as dinner clubs, concerts, picnics out in the sun, or just afternoons playing in the park.

Travel and exploration

Exploring the world allows you to open yourself up to new opportunities and expand into a higher energy level. Go at your own pace and create meaningful experiences that focus on what's most important to you. You can create a set itinerary, but be mindful to leave room for spontaneous moments and enjoy whatever may come.

Overall, your masculine side calls you to step up and take life by the horns. You are the one that has to own your journey and prioritize the time you have as special. Allow yourself some time to lean into the bright side of life and go fully toward your dreams and what makes you feel most alive. You're the one that has to justify whether you spent your time wisely.

BENEFITS AND RESULTS OF FIRE ENERGY

The benefits of fire energy can be really incredible depending on how strongly you lean into this side of yourself. This is where the real tangible pieces of your life come together through hard work and continuing to make progress one step at a time. It's where you see the plans, ideas, and dreams that you've held in your mind and in your heart manifest out in the world and become a reality. When this happens, you're creating your own destiny and taking charge of your present and future. This can be a powerful feeling when you know you're in charge of your life. It can fuel your soul to feel exactly how you want to feel because of your accomplishments. So a great deal of confidence and abundance is created when you show up fully in this way to make things happen.

One of the biggest benefits of fire energy is that you create pride in yourself and in what you've achieved when you go out and do something important to you. You establish alignment in this process, and your mind, body, and spirit work together to allow you to live your best life. Now, the sense of pride that is cultivated from this is not just a means of feeding your ego. Rather, it's a higher vibration that feeds your soul and brings you in tune with your personal power in relation to universal energy. You are a powerful being that moves through life alongside the energies of nature. When you learn to harness your part in that creation energy, you step into your role as a manifestor of what your life is supposed to be.

From this aspect of becoming a creator, there's a much greater sense of satisfaction with how you see your journey taking shape. People often get caught up in feeling like life is happening to them, that life has dealt them a bad hand, or that they just can't seem to be where they want to be. The moment you shift your energy to a place of intentional action, you become a manifestor and take your life in your own hands. By doing that, each moment becomes meaningful. Each milestone shows you are living in alignment and that you are already creating the life you want in the present, not just for a future endpoint. This can significantly transform your perspective on life in order to deepen your personal awareness of your capabilities, your strength, and your energetic ability to maneuver through anything life throws at you.

Clearly, as you become the manifestor of your life, you get closer and closer to the life vision you ultimately have for yourself. With each action, you will align another piece of the puzzle, but your sense of self will also change along the way. You may see yourself in a whole new light as a person who can improve their circumstances and live a happy life on their own terms. Things may also change in your relationships because you're showing up with more confidence, conviction, and personal power. The way you enjoy life may be different as you open up to new opportunities and allow yourself to embrace them.

The world is so expansive, and it becomes available to you when you open yourself up. Fear will diminish bit by bit, and you'll have a freer mentality guiding you out of your comfort zone and into doing things that surprise, excite, and challenge you. This is part of playing full out and feeling like you've lived to the fullest. Your fire energy will call you to do all that you're meant to do and finally break you away from the constraints of your mind and push you to grow wings and fly.

BEST TIMES FOR FIRE ENERGY

These intense fire cycles generate really active, engaged energy. This is not the time to sit on the sidelines and observe. You need to get out there and put your best self into whatever you're doing so you can live fully and create the change, progress, or growth that you need. I've found these moments are sometimes planned, but also many are unplanned. You may have many goals you want to achieve from the life plans you made in the air cycles. Maybe you've planned to start a business, write a book, learn yoga, or do many other things. When you've predetermined what actions are best for you to engage in, those need to go straight on the calendar to ensure you've set aside the time. Devoting specific time frames to them will ensure you've held the space to be consistent and commit your energy to them.

Then, sometimes spontaneity must take over, and you won't be able to plan when fire energy may strike. There could be a spur-of-the-moment thing where you'll have to work up the courage to make a big speech in front of a large crowd or take the leap to tell someone how you really feel. These moments are the ones where you'll have to dig deep, find the strength within yourself from who you know yourself to be, and just jump feet first off the cliff and into your life. We learn the most and grow to the highest levels of ourselves in these times, and they can be the most important ones of our lives. Do your best not to deny yourself of these moments because they're the ones that shape our souls and define our journeys. If we ever lose moments like these, then we lose ourselves.

So, what should you do if you can't plan all of your actions? Well, you can get tapped into your solar plexus energy to embrace life and actively enjoy it. Focus on balancing your third chakra point by standing in your power, making decisions that feel aligned to you, and giving yourself a solid structure of core values from which you'll be able to be your authentic self when life challenges you. From there, it's your responsibility to always act out of self-respect and intention to learn, grow, and improve yourself and the world. If you can say that you're showing up to do those things, then you don't have to worry about anything else. The right opportunities will find you, and you'll answer their call when the time is right.

As for the actions that you can plan, do them in the timing that's right for you. Don't rush through every single goal all at once. Give yourself enough grace to have seasons or cycles to work through whatever truly inspires. Let your heart guide you on which projects you should take on and when. Be practical about how much you can really do at one time and give yourself a reasonable amount of time to accomplish each thing. Stick to small, incremental steps and amounts of time devoted to whatever activity or project you're working on. This way, you'll be giving yourself the best chance for success as you maintain your focus and keep your motivation up for a period that makes sense to you. It could be two weeks when you have some down time from everything else, or it could be six months when you devote yourself to an extensive project. You get to decide what timing feels right. You can experiment with the length of time you set aside for different things until you know what most aligns with the way you like to work or take action.

Also, even though the traditional fire season is summer, don't be afraid to go outside of that time frame. You can certainly devote your summers to adventure, social activities, and anything else that makes you feel alive. After all, the days are the longest and the sun shines most fully for us all to enjoy. However, also realize that fire cycles can and should come throughout the entire year because your growth should never stay stagnant for too long. It takes action to create growth in some capacity, so there will likely always be times throughout the year for you to work on something important to you and your growth. Don't disregard these times just because they may appear inopportune on the surface. If you feel called to have a season where you're striving for something or pushing for the next level, then listen to that call and make it your fire season. You can always come back to claim the fire of summer when it comes around, but you may not have another chance to "seize the day" when the moment presents itself.

fire

FIRE AFFIRMATIONS AND CORRESPONDENCES

Use the following correspondences and affirmations to tap into your fire energy regularly. The energy of these will support you in aligning with your inner power and raising your vibration to a level of awareness that activates your motivations and authentic self. You can carry these with you as you work on your projects or do certain activities, or you can use them alongside meditations, mind/body movement practices, or even in your daily routines to add a punch of masculine energy.

Chakra: Solar Plexus

Moon Phase: Waxing Moon up to the Full Moon

Intentions: Courage, confidence, determination, motivation, purpose

Colors: Yellow, orange

Crystals: Citrine, tiger's eye, honey calcite, pyrite, topaz, amber

Foods: Yellow peppers, pineapple, lemon, turmeric, ginger

Scents: Lemon, lemongrass, chamomile, bergamot, juniper, frankincense, cardamom

Yoga poses: Plank, warrior I and II, bow pose, crescent pose, mountain pose, camel pose

Affirmations:

I am confident in my abilities to navigate my life with strength and purpose.

I achieve the goals that are aligned with my heart and soul.

I am aligned with who I am at my core.

My life has purpose and direction.

I am being intentional in my decisions and my actions.

I am empowered to make decisions from a place of conviction and strength.

I embrace and open myself up to new opportunities in my life.

I enjoy my life fully and allow myself to experience all that I can.

I know who I am and am confident in what feels aligned for me.

I am responsible for my actions and my journey.

I diligently work on the goals that will get me to where I want to be.

I manifest my desires into reality by taking consistent action.

I align my energy with where I want my life to go.

I am in control of my life and where I want it to go.

I am motivated by my personal values and priorities and I make decisions based on those.

I look at my life with positivity and opportunity.

I can achieve all that I set out to do.

Keep in mind that you gain authentic power from within. You are the one that can activate your potential, and no one can take that away from you unless you allow them to. Breathe into your inner knowing as you align with these affirmations and correspondences, and let your inner light emanate out for the world to see.

VISUALIZATION FOR FIRE ENERGY

When you can take a few moments to yourself, sit quietly and focus on your breath. Pay attention to your chest rising and falling with each breath. In each inhale, you are taking in life force energy that fuels all of your cells and activates your body. Bring your awareness to your solar plexus at the very center of your torso. This is the point where you cultivate that life force within you. It's the seat of your inner power and authentic self.

Allow yourself to go into your mind's eye for a moment. Envision yourself outside in a beautiful field of yellow sunflowers. Their heads droop to the side and appear to just linger in the field as if waiting for something. You stroll through the tall stems and feel the clouds parting above you. Streaks of sunlight emerge between the clouds, and the sunflowers slowly shift their heads to align with the awakening sun.

You raise your chin to the sky and feel the warm sunlight on your face. Your arms stretch out to the sides as if to acknowledge the incredible light streaming down upon you amidst the rows and rows of sunflowers. You feel a sense of strength and inner power in this moment, as the light seems to permeate your whole being and fill you with energy.

The sun fades now, and you move your arms down slowly as you take a moment to find gratitude for this sense of personal power within you. Just like the sunflowers, the light has given you the motivation to shift and align with the best direction for your growth. You are ready now to move forward in your own life by tapping into the light within you and letting it guide you.

Slowly you walk through the sunflower field, feeling the tall stalks around you as you brush past them. You have a soft smile on your face as you gently allow yourself to come back to where you are. You breathe deeply into your belly for a moment and come back to the present.

Life Design Action Steps
Fire Energy

1. Make a list of all the values and beliefs that you currently hold. Go through each one to determine where it originated and if it's something that you'd like to continue carrying with you as a core personal value in the next cycle of your life.

2. Identify your top 3-5 personal core values and beliefs that will shape your life. Decide how you will incorporate these into your daily life or at regular

intervals to keep you in alignment with your most authentic self.

3. Come up with an affirmation that aligns with the current season of life that you're in and relates to the goals you have presently. Ensure the statement is a positive way to make you feel empowered and aligned to the intentions you have in your heart for who you want to be.

4. Establish one or two small and measurable action steps that are a priority for you in achieving a major goal. Decide on a time frame for when you will implement these first couple of action steps, set aside time on your calendar to work on them, and keep a progress log as you take intentional action. Check in with yourself halfway through your time frame to see if your energy still feels aligned with these steps and the outcome you're focused on achieving.

5. Plan a couple of activities that will allow you to explore, learn, or get out of your comfort zone for a while. Mark them off on your calendar and coordinate so that all the logistics are in place for you to take this time to enjoy yourself and expand your horizons a bit.

---

1. Ellis, Keith. (1996). The Magic Lamp: Goal Setting For People Who Hate Setting Goals. New York: Three Rivers Press.
2. Ellis, Keith. (1996). The Magic Lamp: Goal Setting For People Who Hate Setting Goals. New York: Three Rivers Press.

3. Ferriss, Timothy. (2007). The 4-Hour Work Week: Escape 9-5, Live Anywhere, and Join The New Rich. New York: Harmony Books.

4. Bernstein, Gabrielle. (2019). Super Attractor: Methods For Manifesting a Life Beyond Your Wildest Dreams. Carlsbad, CA: Hay House, Inc.

5. Harney, Jason (2022). Five Studies Highlighting The Power of Intrinsic Motivation [Blog Page]. Retrieved in April 2022, from https://www.workstars.com/recognition-and-engagement-blog/2020/02/24/5-studies-highlighting-the-power-of-intrinsic-motivation/

6. Harney, Jason (2022). Five Studies Highlighting The Power of Intrinsic Motivation [Blog Page]. Retrieved in April 2022, from https://www.workstars.com/recognition-and-engagement-blog/2020/02/24/5-studies-highlighting-the-power-of-intrinsic-motivation/

7. Shetty, Jay. (2020). Think Like A Monk. New York: Simon & Schuster.

8. Shetty, Jay. (2020). Think Like A Monk. New York: Simon & Schuster.

9. Shetty, Jay. (2020). Think Like A Monk. New York: Simon & Schuster.

Encourage
the gratitude
of your future self
for what
your present self
starts creating
today.

Flow With Life

Fall is a time of satisfaction
For the accomplishments of growth having been achieved
And we can now embrace the release and surrender of a completed progression

We are exactly as we need to be
There is beauty in what we are and how we have evolved
But nothing is permanent

And through change, we may flow through life with better regard for our own state of perfection
Exactly as we are, no matter what that is
Just allowing ourselves to be

In pure joy and pure appreciation for what lies within
And what parts of us need to be nurtured before drawing them out
Into the light once again

aligning water

Chapter Five

Water Energy

The beauty of life comes from complexity and simplicity all rolled into one. If you choose to look at it solely from the view of structure and order, then you'll miss the underlying currents of ease and flow. We're trying to create more moments of harmony in our lives. Hence, it's important to see those underlying currents and embrace them. Often, we try to establish a sense of control through what we can manipulate. Yet, by moving with life, we can actually gain the most control over ourselves and the contentment that we feel. If you think you may have lost this flow somewhere along the way, then it's time to come back to the knowledge that you can be in sync with life and allow it to support you in finding more moments of release and joy.

When I was in my twenties, I left my military job. I remember sitting on our guest bed a few days later, pulling out all of my scrapbooking supplies. I dragged out patterned papers, stamps, fancy tapes, and everything else previously tucked away and only used a handful of times before. I hadn't had the time to dig into any real creative work since I'd been in college. Now I had an indeterminate amount of days in front of me to play with, and I felt so ready to get back to being my creative self again.

For those years, when I was in the military, I was feeding my masculine energy side. It was the side of me that liked structure, order, and getting things done. I stuck to a hectic schedule. I followed procedures, checked the boxes, and worked my way through everything methodically. Yet, it never really made me feel whole because I was always craving the creative side of me underneath. I missed getting to dream up ideas for new houses like I did in school or curate a beautiful event like I did for our wedding. While in the Air Force, that time in my life just made the gap more pronounced from how I had been living to who I truly knew myself to be.

So when I left the military, there was this incredible need to rebalance the feminine side of myself. Within days of leaving, I created more than I had in the last several years of my life. I made cards and scrapbooks, and I fully allowed myself to feel into that moment where I could let my inspiration take me wherever it wanted to go. All at once, my creative side came pouring back to me, and I immersed myself in those moments with joy and complete contentment, without regard for the practicalities of where life would take me in the next season. It didn't really matter because all I needed was to replenish my soul and feel like I was coming back to myself again. It was like I had been wandering through the desert and had finally reached a massive water source.

This is the power of water energy. It submerges you in the feminine side of yourself to connect deeply to your emotions, intuition, creativity, and flow. It's the side of us that balances out the practicality of the masculine and links us more to the yearnings of our souls and our most heartfelt desires. When we tap into the feminine with the water element, we're embracing the unique parts of ourselves, including those we may feel we've suppressed or hidden away.

As you align with this energy, having grace for yourself is important. There's so much that may come to the surface and rise within you, and it's okay to acknowledge every part of yourself that you find. Emotions are part of who we are, and through cultivating our inner world, we become more in tune with ourselves, our truth, and our place in life. That will give us more awareness as we move forward along our paths. The most important thing is to not be afraid of whatever comes up for you. Allow yourself to lean into your shadow side with the things you may have repressed. Uncover what lies underneath the surface. Be willing to recognize your desires and your inspiration. Follow those paths without hesitation and let your soul discover itself again by letting go of all the judgments or expectations to just be fully you.

Now is the time to dance in the rain, sing in the shower, run naked through your backyard, talk to your spirit guides, and spend the afternoon getting lost in something that's pure joy for you. There are no limitations here with water energy, only self-expression and bliss that allow you to flow with life in a way that fills your soul and nurtures the depths of who you are. It may seem difficult to go all in with this deeply emotional energy at first, especially if you're used to living for to-do lists and checking boxes. Once you lean into it little by little, you may discover the world becomes fuller, and your experience of it amplifies from the beauty you find within and alongside yourself.

This chapter will guide you in developing your own powerful water energy. Use this as your inspiration to follow your heart over your head and know that all of the answers you need lie inside you. Give yourself time to try different practices and find the most aligned ways of working this water energy into your life. You may find that some aspects of it resonate with you more than others, so be mindful of that and choose the ones that make sense with the lifestyle you want to create. Overall, this element is about the soul-centered side of yourself and how life is supposed to be enjoyed every step of the way. So find your joy within these spaces and seek as many moments of water energy as you can.

LEANING INTO YOUR INTUITION

The first step in discovering your feminine side is to listen to your inner guidance more fully. We each have a voice inside of us that supports us throughout life, and that voice comes from our higher selves, spirit guides, ancestors, higher vibrational energies, and the universal energy we're all connected to. It's important to develop a relationship with this internal voice and allow that to be your first point of guidance before anything else. Because this inner voice is a deep expression of higher consciousness, it steers us in a direction that's for our highest good. When we are open to receiving this insight, life happens synchronously for us in ways we couldn't imagine otherwise.

So as you tap into your intuition, you're connecting to yourself and a higher vibration on a soul-centric level, which is so much deeper than just making decisions based on the practicalities of life through our minds. Here we're acknowledging that there's something beyond practicality at work and that you internally understand where and who you're meant to be. It just needs to come to the surface through your intuition. That's the universal energy at work within you, aligning you to your best life. Trusting this guidance will also be much more fruitful than if you were to follow any instructions from others or society, because it roots you in your most authentic self.

Author and spiritual teacher Sonia Choquette says, "Choosing to accept and embrace help from higher sources means leaving behind the old life of fear and lack of control. Those who do leave, at least from my experience, have a far more blessed, synchronistic, abundant, joyful life."[1] This is where we need to allow the universe to work in our favor. By opening yourself up to this higher guidance, you're letting go enough to have more control over your inner awareness and the connection you have with life itself. The illusion of fear will subside because you're no longer blinded by what you're unaware of in life. You will have guidance. A deeper understanding of what lies within your heart emerges, and you will establish a more enlightened perspective from which to draw upon when you tap into this intuitive energy.

Knowing this, how can you pay more attention to your intuition? First, several things deter us from following our intuition. That could include listening to outside sources telling us what has worked for them or what we should do. We end up thinking they know best when, in reality, those things may not really align for us. Other times, you may get stuck between different ideas because you're afraid to make the wrong decision. In these ways, we can push ourselves away from our intuition and try to do things by thinking them through as much as we can. We stay in our head space and keep thinking that's the best way to solve our dilemmas. However, doing that can actually get in the way and prevent us from hearing what lies within our hearts. So we must make the space to reduce the noise around us and within our own minds in order to pay more attention to what's in our hearts. We need to drop into our heart center, and be more aware of what our feelings are already telling us.

The other question that we need to address upfront is how you can tell the difference between intuition and fear. Your intuition will speak to you out of love, positivity, truth, and expansiveness. It's never out of fear, worry, doubt, or contraction. It won't be restrictive. Rather, your intuition will support you in becoming the best version of yourself. Even if your inner voice tells you that a situation is bad for you, your intuition will lead you down a path of love rather than doing something because you're afraid of the consequences or results.

Also, it's important to realize that everyone has this intuitive voice within them, and you just need to practice listening and figuring out how your own intuition works for you. It's a matter of discerning how it comes across and slowly paying attention to the ways you notice it. Start with the little things and work your way up to the bigger ones. That way, you'll be able to spot the best way to receive messages from your guidance in a low-stakes environment that will give you the confidence to trust it in critical situations.

As you pay attention, you may notice a variety of different things. Sometimes you may be able to decide on doing something instantly. Other times, you may think about doing something randomly when you least expect it. You could walk through a bookstore, and that environment could spark the idea that you should write a book. It may seem random, but when a thought comes up that feels really aligned and raises your energy level, you should pay attention.

Your feelings may also change in an instant. Perhaps you immediately feel excitement or even stress over the thought of something. You experience a swift change in your energetic state of being, which could even trigger a body sensation such as lightness, loosening, tension, or tightness. They could tell you to go all in on something or to avoid it completely, depending on your feelings. You may also have audible messages in your mind or aloud that occur in your own voice, another voice, or with sounds such as music to be your signal. Visions in your mind's eye are another way that you could get an automatic download of information. It could even play out as a movie in your mind or a quick glimpse into what you need to know.

Whatever way your intuition comes across, you can practice paying attention and slowly becoming more aware when it's happening. The more you recognize these moments, the more attuned you'll become to receiving them. When you're open to it, come out of your mind for a moment and tap in. Remove yourself from the need to work through your thoughts and process everything. You can do that later, but when you're receiving insight, just observe what's in your heart and become a vessel for that download. Showing up from a heart space, the answers will come to you, and you'll instantaneously realize what you need to know and feel.

That's not to say that you won't have any hesitation throughout this process, though, and that's okay. In her book, Ask Your Guides, Choquette brings this up by saying, "Living an intuitive, six-sensory, guided life takes courage. The guides will point out the best way to fulfill your path and purpose and make day-to-day life easier, but it's still up to you to decide whether to follow their input."[2] You always have the choice, and it's with that choice that comes your personal power. So it's just a matter of finding the trust you need within yourself to know you are being supported and that the energy within you and surrounding you have your best interests at heart. If you're willing to test your higher guidance out and lean into it little by little, chances are you'll find it's the most important instruction you ever receive throughout your life.

To support you in making this a practice, you can keep an intuition journal. Write any times when you feel or sense your intuition at work. At first, try to do this with little things such as what you'll have for dinner that night. Lean into your intuition to guide you toward what you're feeling, such as whether you'd like spaghetti or roast chicken. You'll just naturally have a moment where something will come to you and feel great. The same goes for when you get dressed in the morning. Let your energy guide you in deciding what to wear by how you feel. You probably do these things most days without even thinking about them, and that's the point. Start where you are and expand as you become more aware. This way, you'll have more moments where you're checking in with yourself and seeing how you feel about something naturally without going straight into your head.

Record as much as you can within your journal, and then, over time, you can apply your new awareness to bigger situations and decisions. You'll be able to go back and see any patterns from your journal and identify if you receive feelings more often or if you have a clear knowing about something. Then, you'll have established a greater energetic connection to your higher self, allowing you to drop into your heart space more quickly and easily and directly get the insights you need more consistently. Remember, you have the answers within your soul already. The more you tap into those, the more aligned your life will become. It's just a matter of being open and setting the intention to receive. After that, have trust in yourself enough to move through life using this guidance and releasing the fear that's holding you back from doing so. If you can do this, the world will slowly open up, and you'll be moving through life with more vision, joy, and contentment than ever before.

FINDING YOUR CREATIVE INSPIRATION

As I hinted at at the beginning of this chapter, creative inspiration is a huge aspect of this feminine water energy. With creativity, you can easily allow yourself to access the depths of your soul and pull out emotions to be expressed fully into material form. Elizabeth Gilbert, the author of the book, *Big Magic*, relates that, "The universe buries strange jewels deep within us all, and then stands back to see if we can find them."[3] Your chance to find these jewels is through the willingness to let your creative expression run wild. Of course, this can be done through any medium that calls to you, including writing, speaking, visual arts, design, crafts, or any means where you create something from your self-expression and manifest a contribution to the world.

Writer Neil Gaiman says, "We all have an obligation to daydream. We have an obligation to imagine. It is easy to pretend that nobody can change anything, that society is huge and the individual is less than nothing. But the truth is individuals make the future, and they do it by imagining that things can be different."[4] Showing up to let your imagination guide you is an exercise in expanding your own perspective, but also the world's. Each time you open the floodgates of your mind and heart by bringing something into existence that challenges people, moves them with emotion, captivates minds, or makes someone widen their eyes with curiosity, you have done a great service to your soul and theirs. Only creativity can expose our hearts in this way and enlighten us on a deep enough level to expose the truths of our lives. That is worth taking the time to cultivate regularly.

And not only does creative expression give us the chance to open up, but we can do this by mimicking the energy of creation. Through this process, you're taking on the archetypal energy of Mother Earth creating life and the universe in bringing something into emergence from nothing. That same energy is within you, and as you release your inspiration, you can use that to fuel your greatest expressions and become the vessel for the universe to speak from. This is where the beauty of our own transformation emerges. As Gaiman suggests, we cannot see things differently until we create something different. It has to emerge out of a spark of inspiration. Everything comes from this, and as we create, our perspectives develop in a way that shifts the entire world for us. That's an incredible gift if we're willing to embrace it and feel the expansiveness that birthing a new viewpoint on life can bring.

So when you step into your water energy, allow yourself to dive into any creative endeavors that call to you. Don't be afraid to set aside the to-do list and spend time on any hobbies or passions that may evoke a sense of curiosity in you. Give yourself space one day a week or perhaps in the evenings to do something that makes you feel really inspired and motivated to see whatever comes out of you. It's time to let your ideas run wild and enjoy the abandon you can feel as you show up unrestrained by anything other than your own muse.

One of the biggest ways that you can more consciously tap into that muse is by choosing a time each day to connect with it consistently. Gilbert talks about the idea of coming back to a regular time where you pay attention to your muse and focus on being creative, you're telling your muse that the door is open for whatever insight is ready to come through.[5] You're there waiting for it and willing to be a vessel for the messages that need to enlighten the world. So it's almost like setting up a regular appointment with yourself and your higher guidance so you're fully present and letting everything else go in favor of creative expression. When you think about it, this really brings you directly back to the intention of opening your heart regularly. Nothing else will be there to distract you, and you're just finding the time to allow for heart-centered moments where you can immerse yourself in a higher vibration and share that with the world.

Now alongside consciously tapping in regularly, this idea of cultivating your muse does require you to be genuine and raw. If you hold back, not saying all that you want to say, then there's some shadow work that needs to be uncovered. Maybe you have some limiting beliefs or there could be some doubts, fears, or expectations getting in the way. This time should bring you back to your wild woman's side where you're unafraid to howl at the moon and throw abandon to the wind. As Gilbert says," A creative life is an amplified life, and a hell of a lot more interesting life. Living in this manner— continually and stubbornly bringing forth the jewels that are hidden within you— is a fine art, in and of itself."[6] There's no place for constraints of fear and doubt unless it's purely to expose them and work through them artistically so you may unearth those jewels of your soul. Otherwise, the more you can shed the limitations that put a muzzle on your inner voice, the more free you'll feel and the more you'll experience the full expansiveness of creative living.

FOLLOWING YOUR BLISS

Going hand in hand with expressing yourself creatively is also allowing yourself time to follow what makes you feel alive and joyful. This could be anything from going on a spontaneous trip with a partner to choosing a career that lights you up rather than one that's just for the money. The highest level of energy that you can live at is one where you are in complete bliss. Now this is something that is extremely transient in our lives and that we usually only reach when we get into a complete state of joy and connection with ourselves and the world. In the times that people actually do fully reach this state, we call it enlightenment. It's definitely a significant journey of the soul to get there, though, and one that most of us are still learning to experience. So we have to embrace as many moments of our bliss as we can to achieve this state where we feel totally at peace and completely one with where we are in the moment.

That energy of peaceful existence is what we can expect when we follow our bliss. Think about how you feel when doing your absolute favorite activities. The rest of the world probably melts away, and you have less stress, anxiety, or worry at those points in time. The more you say "yes" to things that bring you into that kind of energetic state, the more you raise your vibration and create a greater awareness of how life source energy exists within and around you. It becomes a more positive experience, and the lower vibrations can't exist on the same level any longer because your perspective has changed.

Happiness and joy are essential to living a conscious, balanced life. They're not just frivolous ways to spend your time. They're some of the most important ways to use your time because they'll put you in a state of being that surpasses any of our societally-dictated ideas of success and happiness. Instead, you'll be creating peace within yourself from what actually brings you the highest joy. This is all because you will have experienced the joys of being in your bliss and seeing that surrounding you more often.

NURTURING YOURSELF ALONG THE WAY

When we think about creating balance in our lives, we tend to seek more self-care practices that can compensate for the overwork we've already put ourselves through. Let's be honest about this one. If you're at the point where you're completely burnt out and all you can think about is how a hot bath or a trip to the spa would refresh your energy, then you're most likely already way past the point of being in alignment. That's when you know it's definitely time to make some changes. So you'll want to consider how you may have let your masculine side take over and how that hint of a hot bath is actually a signal to take a deeper look at how you care for yourself.

To start, self-care is so much more than putting a spa appointment on your calendar every once in a while. It's about creating harmony in your mind, body, and soul so that you feel like your cup is full in a more holistic sense. While that's really what we're trying to do in embracing every elemental energy here, your water energy, in particular, is where this really draws your attention to the soul aspect underneath everything else. It's where you're nurturing the emotions that lie underneath your mindset and your physical presence. It's what brings everything together and ensures that you're honoring yourself as a beautiful compilation of many dimensions of your soul. And in order to do this, you can find practices that cater to the needs of each aspect of yourself.

Self-care advocate and author, Tenae Stewart, suggests we think of this as "care of your inner self through nourishment of your mental and emotional health and the care of your outer self through nourishment of your physical body."[7] Plus, she suggests that we also identify self-care that comes from within us and "self-care that comes from outside of ourselves, from the natural world or the divine."[8] It's not only about meeting our needs independently, but also tapping into the power of life force energy that continually surrounds us in order to invigorate our souls. That energy is there within Mother Earth, the people in our lives, and even in the elements themselves, such as the air we breathe, to sustain us and give us exactly what we need to maintain life.

So we can approach self-care from these many angles and allow it to take shape in many forms in our lives. Depending on personal preferences, these forms could include journaling, coaching, or deep conversations with friends to care for your mental health. It could mean practicing yoga on your deck every morning to wake up your body with fresh air and put you in a state of ease for the day. Perhaps it's about developing a walking meditation practice or even taking a tarot reading class to improve your spiritual awareness and gain a heightened state of consciousness. Many things can feel nurturing as long as they are giving you a feeling of filling your energetic cup back up so that it doesn't dip too low. You want to show up in your life with a sense of positivity and satisfaction so that you're ready to approach whatever comes with a clear mind and an open heart. Doing this takes an approach to self-care that touches on several levels of who you are and occurs through accepting, appreciating, and aligning with your entire self.

Journaling is one of the biggest activities that I suggest to people because it gives you the space to connect with your holistic needs. It allows you to tap into your inner guidance, discover what needs to come to the surface, and it provides the means for therapeutically working through things in a safe space. But this is just one means to an end. Ultimately, the intention is to find the space to nurture every aspect of yourself. So often, we give ourselves to everyone else and all we do in the world, leaving nothing for what we need. Yet, it's in self-compassion that we can brighten our light to shine more intensely outward in the world.

I suggest that you choose activities that aren't focused on taking care of just one aspect of yourself, but many. Look at what you truly enjoy doing that will satisfy your mind. That could include reading regularly or taking classes. Find things that will keep your body feeling its best, such as new eating plans or mindful movement exercises. Join communities or activities that will increase your enjoyment and fuel your soul like creative organizations or spiritual groups. These things play a role in the energy that you feel daily, and you'll be nurturing the life force energy within you as you do them.

This is how you approach self-care from the standpoint of healing and restoring health rather than just putting a bandaid over something that's bleeding. Your whole self must feel the impact of this Mother Earth energy in order to benefit from it in every aspect of your life. Not to mention that you also take care of the collective energy as you do this for yourself. Self-care for the mind is self-care for collective wisdom. For the body, it's care for our collective presence here on Earth. And for your soul, it's care for the oneness of energy that is all things. It may seem like it's all about you and making yourself feel better, but in the much larger picture of life, when you heal yourself, you heal the world. Everyone shares in our universal energy. Each time you lift a part of yourself higher, the entire consciousness gets lifted alongside you.

So if you're feeling at all selfish about taking time to care for yourself, then just know that it isn't really about you at all. You're supporting humanity and all that exists. When you align with a more holistic way of being, you're stepping into your heart center once again and activating the part of you that grows with love and kindness. That is the ultimate way that we can be present in our lives, and there's nothing more respectable and selfless than the purity of showing up with love.

GOING WITH THE FLOW OF LIFE

One last aspect of feminine energy that aligns with the water element is the concept of flow. If you think about how water moves, it maneuvers its way around anything by transforming and reshaping itself to flow around whatever surrounds it. And yet, through it all, it maintains itself and stays true to what it naturally is. This is the idea of flow we should all incorporate into our lives. There's so much uncertainty around us, and we can't control all the happenings of life, no matter how hard we try. All we can do is control our inner thoughts, emotions, and actions. Through those things, we can stay true to ourselves and align our energy in ways that move us through life fluidly and naturally in alignment.

Your journey through life should be beautiful and joyful, and to create this type of happiness, you must show up by first letting go. So this is the cycle where you can embody that fluidity of water by being mindful of who you are and letting go of any ideas of control or resistance. Think about the trees as they lose their leaves in the fall. They're releasing the need to stay attached when it's time to just let go. Perhaps they understand the cycles that must occur, or they're allowing themselves to just "be." They're being who they're meant to be in the flow of the moment and the cycle they're in. It's solely about existing for them at that point in time.

Having the flow of water means you must learn to just "be" and be okay with that. There's no denying how difficult it can be to do this, but through accepting whatever life brings, you allow for more peace in your life. There is less resistance and more freedom to be present and aware, which aligns you naturally with the person you are. The act of trying to dictate our lives constantly and force ourselves to follow a specific path is just attracting tension and stress. That's basically what force does. So why would we want to create more of that in our lives? By practicing more acceptance, we free ourselves from this constant cycle of tension and choose more peace and joy.

At a point in my life, I had to dig deep to embrace this philosophy of letting go. We had just lost our second child during pregnancy, and it was difficult to come to terms with what had happened. In those initial moments, I felt numb and totally distant from life as I was experiencing it. Yet, as the days passed, I knew I had a choice to make. I could either perceive myself as a victim to life and go into a place where I felt no control over what was happening to me, or I could choose to alter my perspective and see this as life giving me a gift. It was one of the hardest seasons of my life, but I chose the latter and learned some of the greatest lessons that life presented to me.

I found I didn't have to look at life from a victim's perspective, but that I could see the lessons of unconditional love, surrender, acceptance, and limitless connection to move me forward. I could step into my power and find a deeper meaning in this situation and understand myself better. It didn't happen overnight. I remember crying on the floor as my toddler watched me and asked what the matter was. He didn't fully understand what happened, but he could feel my energy. I knew in those moments there would be gifts to help me grow and come out of this as a higher version of myself. Plus, I knew I had to find and embrace those things for not only myself but for my husband and son to move forward with peace.

There was so much shadow work that came up. I had a great deal about myself that I had to uncover and work through. Yet I chose not to resist what life put in front of me. I dug into the emotion, sat with its rawness, and elevated my thinking to find gratitude in an otherwise difficult and heartbreaking situation. Then, I anchored myself to my beautiful son and the person I wanted to be for him. Honoring my power over my thoughts, feelings, and actions, I used them to propel me forward with love and appreciation. From that experience, I completely broke open my view of the world and put it back together in a way that raised me to the next level of my growth.

Pain is something that may be part of your journey as well, but it's something that doesn't have to overtake you. Bernstein says, "The shift for me was that I decided to stop giving purpose to my pain. I honored my suffering from the past but chose not to dwell in it. I decided to be new and accept joy as my birthright."[9] You can claim the pain to show you a new path forward, rather than wallowing in it. Any pain you feel can become your greatest strength if you allow it to. It can direct you where to let more light into your soul and let go of the resistance you feel. It's only one emotional connection to our reality, but it's a powerful one that has the potential to give you moments of complete surrender.

Bernstein also states, "When we embody an energy of joy, we release resistance. I recognize that it can be difficult to find joy in seemingly joyless situations, but it's far more painful to live a joyless existence. So many of us inadvertently live that way, whether by focusing on what's not working or by frequently complaining about our circumstances. We hope complaining will make us feel better or at least help us find a sympathetic ear. But when we focus on what's not working, we just get more of what's not working."[10] Yet when we transform that pain and resistance into an energy of gratitude and joy, we become more in tune with life's many other blessings. From there, the light you've let in becomes the beacon for much more light to come.

This said, flow isn't just about accepting pain to overcome it and move on. The intention is to surrender to all the currents of life, not just pain and discomfort, but everything that comes our way. Doing this creates a deeper inner stability and awareness to follow a path more in tune with our higher selves than we could have ever realized before, even through sudden pain, complete surprises, or ongoing challenges. This is going to take some practice, though. We can't just get to a point where we fully accept life as it is in one fail swoop. However, it is doable with little steps, just as you did by using your intuition and working your way up to bigger things. This could look like you starting by letting go of whatever the weather does and how it may affect your plans. Maybe you let go of the frustration you have previously felt if someone canceled an appointment with you.

Observe the moments of life that seem to test you. Look at them in the larger context of life and how one small thing does not define your entire path. Try to embrace the mindset of what you can control with your thoughts, emotions, and actions and reshape the situation from a place of personal power. Being flexible and creating more flow is about being willing to shift, especially in the moment. So practice seeing the alternate paths available to you just as water does when it encounters something blocking its way.

Slowly, as you find acceptance for the occurrences of life, you can look at those bigger things. For instance, consider how you can maintain your own sense of inner stability even when the world around you leans to the negative or seems to fall apart at the seams. You can be the river that moves around the boulders and stone outcroppings of life and even pours down the cliff edge, only to come right back into a calm pool at the bottom. Remember, you are not beholden to the circumstances of life. In actuality, your life's circumstances are supporting you. The energy you're putting into the universe will attract more of the same to you. By practicing more surrender and flow, you'll be letting go of resistance to the support directed at you and flowing freely rather than crashing up against the rocks.

To bring this full circle, the key to flow in your life is self-responsibility. As we've discussed, there are things in life that are in your control and things that are not. You are a powerful creator of your reality when you see that your thoughts, emotions, and actions dictate reality. Those are the energetic currency that you hold. When you realize this, your path forward becomes your own, no matter what else tries to deter you. And with that self-responsibility comes a great deal of opportunity. You get to decide where you will pivot or shift in life. If something isn't going well or you feel overwhelmed and frustrated, it takes a moment to view where you stand and shift to find a more opportune way forward. In this way, you'll be the water that is constantly moving and adapting to find a better way through.

Now, I want you to try this in your daily interactions, your work, and even with your habits. Shift your point of view slightly when things get rough and find the path that will guide you gracefully forward with strength and agility through the use of your own inner strengths and traits. Use who you are at your soul level to your advantage. Know yourself well enough to see where life is guiding you on a better path and where you may be happier or more in your element.

If you feel like this is too big of an ask for you to handle, then take it one day at a time. You might even want to set aside one day each week where you'll work on going with the flow. It could be a Friday or even a Sunday where you decide to surrender to whatever life brings that day and allow yourself to flow with it. If things feel stressful, that's your cue to implement this process. As you surrender more, you'll find this practice creeping into how you approach all aspects of your life until it's a part of who you've become. I wouldn't expect this to happen over a month, but maybe over a year or two of practice. You could get to a place where you're much more accepting of how life happens and how it benefits you.

ACTIVITIES FOR WATER ENERGY

Getting into a state of flow, ease, and inspiration can be as easy as giving yourself a few moments to enjoy life or it can be a gradual progression of letting go. By choosing a selection of different water element activities, you can get a quick pick-me-up or slowly shift the way you approach your entire life with more grace and happiness. Start where you are and pay attention to your emotions as you go through these activities. Do your best to remove as much judgment as you can and appreciate the time that you spend doing these activities without limitations.

Spiritual Communication

Get to know your spirit guides and your higher guidance better by opening a channel of communication with them.

Set the intention to quiet your mind regularly and tune in to whatever insights they may have for you. It may even be fun to develop a language with your guides around signs, images, sounds, or anything that may give you hints at what you need to pay attention to. You can also keep a journal as you work with your guides to figure out any patterns or signs that occur often.

Shadow Work Journaling

In order to work out what you need to let go of, you can keep a journal of any limiting beliefs, assumptions, judgments, fears, or anything holding you back from living your best life. Identify the beliefs in your journal and work through where they may have come from. Allow yourself to process the experience you've had with these things over time and how they've affected you. Find gratitude for what you've learned through your experiences, and then journal how you may reframe or let go to become the person you now want to be.

Creative Activities

An important part of being our authentic selves is to allow time for free expression. We can do this by tapping into the things that truly inspire us or that we're being guided to develop within ourselves. For example, you may be interested in artwork that's inspired by nature, creating new recipes from international flavors, or even building new bicycles for people of all sizes. The idea here is to allow your imagination and inspiration to transport you away from the practicality of life for a while to manifest something unique into the world that speaks to your soul.

Passion Projects

When we give ourselves the space to take on passion projects, we're saying "yes" to following our hearts and letting our spirits guide us. This puts us closer to bliss at higher energy levels, and we want to cultivate those moments as often as possible. So you could choose to do anything that sets your soul on fire here. You may take the weekends to write the fantasy story you've been dying to write. Finally, take that trip to South America and learn to salsa dance. Choose to spend some time doing the things that make your heart sing so that you let go of expectations and let your passions fuel you.

Self-care Practices

Try to build some rituals and routines into your life that allow you to nurture yourself on many levels. Start with simple things like reading before bed, stretching in the morning, or drinking more water. When you're ready, you may choose to develop a more in-depth practice of meditation, journaling, or even going to regular classes and meetups that support you in mind, body, and spirit.

Listening To Music

Music is something that can lift our spirits and transform our energy in the moment. A song that speaks to our souls can move us in ways that nothing else can. So whenever you get the chance to put on some of your favorite music, go dancing, listen to a live concert, or any other way of enjoying music, then enjoy life, embrace your spirit, and let life flow for a while.

Water element activities are a beautiful expression of your inner self. They can be a great way to honor who you truly are and not just the reflection of yourself that's presented in life. So the more you can bring these activities into your daily lifestyle, the more you will align your actions with your true spirit and emotions.

BENEFITS OF WATER ENERGY

When we think about water, it may seem gentle and easygoing, but in reality, it's incredibly strong and can maneuver through the harshest of landscapes. Think about the crashing rapids that have sliced cracks through giant boulders over time or the raging hurricane waters that have washed away many shorelines. As you allow yourself to become like water, you're going to be activating a side of yourself that has deep inner power and strength. That kind of power must be respected and used intentionally to create the best outcome.

This is the time to step into your natural power with grace and ease rather than pure force. You can use it to listen to yourself above all else and rely on who you are to move through life without being limited by what's around you or other people's perceptions and interpretations of reality. You get to decide what is best for you based on intuition, inspiration, and passion. When you listen to yourself fully, you'll be bringing more ease into your life and things will no longer feel as if you're pushing a boulder uphill.

Your idea of reality will change, too, as you find more of your bliss and see the world at work in your favor rather than being against you. You'll be more open to going after your dreams and goals, taking opportunities as they come to you, and seeing things based on growth and alignment over fear or just practicality. The water within will bring you in tune with your emotions to respect them and your heart. Yet, you can also become capable of using your emotions with more awareness and restraint when necessary, as they will no longer completely overtake you.

Moving through life will have much more pleasure and passion because you'll be doing things that inspire you and feel good. Each day will bring joy and fulfillment and you won't be wondering what else there is to life anymore. You'll have a deeper sense of connection and alignment with each step. It no longer becomes about constantly striving for the next goal to get to the right endpoint. You'll just be flowing, enjoying the journey, and intuitively knowing you're exactly where you're meant to be.

I know that it could feel quite distant and unrealistic if you haven't yet experienced this level of bliss. But the reality is actually that it's completely within your power to achieve this. All you need to do is choose things that make you happy and find some good in the rest. There will always be ways to make things more difficult. If you approach life with more understanding that you create your own happiness, then life will become easier as you make decisions from that standpoint. No one can choose to give you happiness but you. Each moment presents an opportunity to find more joy, more ease, and more flow. It's up to you whether you're willing to embrace it.

BEST TIME FOR WATER ENERGY

In all honesty, the best time for water energy is any moment where you can get tapped into your inner self, your joy, and the connection you have with life. It doesn't have to be at any set time. Although, it can be really helpful to pre-schedule some activities, so you know you'll always have time to come back to what makes you happy. However, the whole point of water energy is to be in flow, to go with the tides of life, and to allow your journey to transpire how it's meant to happen. So whenever you get a sign to stop pushing and start letting go, take it.

That said, I want to cover a few instances where water energy will serve you well. Of course, the first time is the season of fall, which corresponds with the water element. This is the natural time of the year when nature calls us to let go, enjoy the flow of life, and get still to listen to our inner selves as the world slows down. You can take this as a chance to pay more attention to yourself and have a bit more self-care or even time to connect with your spirit guides and ancestors. The energy around us becomes much less heavy at this time of year. So it's the perfect season for raising your vibration to communicate more with higher guidance.

Besides fall, you may also open up to your intuition as you lean into any plans for the future. Ensure your planning aligns with your higher self and what feels right for you. So before putting any project plans into place or implementing your goals, check that you intuitively feel good. Then, you can also practice releasing any expectations, fears, or worries before starting something new. Remember, before each season of growth, make space for something new using your air energy. We also want to bring the water energy in to shed what will no longer serve us in the next cycle of life.

Then, as we work on our goals and go out into the world, it's not all about constantly doing things and getting everything done. That fire energy must be blended with water energy to ensure we maintain our passion and joy. If we're just checking the boxes, there's no real meaning or fulfillment behind it. That's no way to live. So from time to time, in the middle of working on your goals, just come back to yourself and have a check-in moment. Tap into your intuition and your feelings to identify whether you're still satisfied and inspired by what you're doing or whether something may need to change.

Of course, the same is true about checking in after you've worked hard and completed any task. That's when it's time to celebrate your hard work and accomplishments. Give yourself a chance to appreciate yourself for all that you've done. Restore your energy through self-care and replenish your inspiration through new creative endeavors. Giving yourself the space to enjoy life after working hard signals to your subconscious and the universe that you're willing to receive all the abundance that comes to you from the energy you put out. So if you want to bring more abundance into your life, the key is acknowledging what you've already created to magnetize even more.

Finally, spontaneous moments can bring us some of the most joy in our lives. By letting go and allowing ourselves to go with the flow, we can experience a sense of abandon that frees us from any limitations, keeping us in lower vibrations. We can give in to what life is putting in front of us and be willing to enjoy it without feeling guilty. It's about accepting that we are worthy of joy and happiness and that it's okay to receive it. That is the feminine in its purest form of receptivity and acceptance. If you can find moments of absolute acceptance, then peace will be much closer for you to achieve in every aspect of life.

WATER AFFIRMATIONS AND CORRESPONDENCES

You can use the following corresponding objects and affirmations to connect more deeply to your feminine water energy. Use them in your meditations, alongside intuitive guidance, in tarot readings, placed in creative spaces or areas where you practice self-care, and even incorporated into the rituals you establish in your life. The beautiful thing about the correspondences here is that they're meant for whatever purpose and place feels best and most aligned for you. So pay attention to what your heart says and follow it to the right use for you.

Chakra: Sacral
Moon Phase: Full Moon through the Waning Moon
Intentions: Passion, creativity, intuition, higher guidance, self-care, nourishment, bliss, flow, release
Colors: Orange, brown

Crystals: Orange calcite, tiger's eye, citrine, orange jasper, carnelian, sunstone, amber

Foods: Oranges, grapefruits, sweet potatoes, apricots, pumpkin, peaches, carrots, cantaloupe, salmon

Scents: Sandalwood, clove, orange, ylang-ylang, cardamom, nutmeg, ginger

Yoga poses: Goddess pose, crescent pose, low lunge, squat pose, bridge, camel, easy pose

Affirmations:

I enjoy my life and all the pleasures in it.

I am in tune with my emotions and find strength in them.

I allow my creativity to bloom without restraint.

I flow with life and allow it to guide me forward.

I intuitively choose my path through life with an open heart.

I connect with my higher self and inner guidance with every step.

I am open to receiving insight along my path.

I trust my feelings and where they lead me.

I am allowed to find joy and happiness in my life.

I embrace my sexuality as a part of who I am.

I love myself unconditionally.

I choose joy and ease in my life.

I release all that holds me back and find peace in letting go.

I take care of myself in order to live more fully.

I respect my mind, body, and spirit and choose to live in alignment.

The power to see life as a gift is within your capability. You just have to embrace the beauty that is present and available to you by making choices guided by intuition, passion, and a compassionate spirit. All the abundance you're looking for derives from this, and as you see more of how you can create it as you desire, the world will open up for you.

VISUALIZATION FOR WATER ENERGY

Take a few moments where you can get comfortable and sit quietly by yourself. You could play some gentle music or rainstorm nature sounds in the background. Take your time to ease into the moment. Allow your mind to empty from all the happenings of the day and focus on taking slow, soothing breaths.

Then, when you're ready, imagine yourself outside at night, walking up to a gorgeous lake shimmering in the moonlight. The light bathes the ripples of the water as they gently cascade toward you on the shore. You slide your shoes off and set them aside as you watch the ripples on the surface and smile to yourself. Gradually, you lift your gaze toward the sky and raise your hands to the moon as if giving thanks for this moment to connect deeply with yourself and all that surrounds you.

You decide to embrace this chance to wade into the water. With each step, you feel the coolness on your skin and become enveloped in the fluidity around you. You push out into the lake with your arms and legs and then swirl around on your back so you're floating just above the surface. You release all stress into the water and feel the light of the moon softly shining upon you with fresh energy.

You feel pure bliss in this moment as you float gently and allow your body to move with the soft current. You are one with the moon above and the water below. There's incredible ease in this moment as you enjoy drifting without needing to go anywhere. You smile and slowly swim back to the edge of the water.

This time has given you a gift of surrender and joy, and you now have a renewed sense of fulfillment within yourself. You celebrate this moment by putting your hands on your heart center and graciously thanking the moon and the water for what they've given you. As you grab your shoes and turn away to walk back to where you came, your mind, body, and spirit feel inspired to continue your journey. Slowly, you focus on your breath once more and draw your attention to where you are.

You can use this visualization to immerse yourself in the energy of the water and your inner connection to it. Don't be afraid to extend this meditation and see where it takes you. Lean into the qualities of the moon and the lake you hope to possess. Let yourself stay in this environment in your mind's eye for long enough to feel your emotions and experience how it affects you. Use it as a time to practice receiving joy and fulfillment. The more you envision yourself connecting with this type of energy, the more you'll be able to embody it in your life.

Life Design Action Steps
Water Energy

1. Create a conversation with your higher guidance by setting aside a regular time to connect and open yourself up to whatever insights may come through. Develop a language with a few key signs or symbols that your spiritual guides can send you when you need support.

2. Start an intuition journal to track how you receive guidance, insights, or downloads. Review it regularly

to see if you can spot patterns or ways you usually connect with your intuition through thoughts, feelings, visions, or even sounds.

3. Set aside time to do something you're passionate about and let nothing else take priority over this time. Slowly try to increase the time you spend on these passion projects.

4. Decide on at least one activity that nourishes your mind, body, and spirit. Start building each of these into your regular routines and rituals. This can be through morning or evening routines, weekend rituals, or even things you do with friends and family.

5. Practice letting go by choosing one day each week to surrender to whatever life brings. Write your thoughts about how the day goes and any insights that occur.

---

1. Choquette, Sonia (2007). Ask Your Guides: Connecting To Your Divine Support System. Carlsbad, CA: Hay House, Inc.
2. Choquette, Sonia (2007). Ask Your Guides: Connecting To Your Divine Support System. Carlsbad, CA: Hay House, Inc.
3. Gilbert, Elizabeth (2015). Big Magic: Creative Living Beyond Fear. New York: Riverhead Books.
4. Gaiman, Neil (2019). Art Matters: Because Your Imagination Can Change The World. New York: William Morrow.
5. Gilbert, Elizabeth (2015). Big Magic: Creative Living Beyond Fear. New York: Riverhead Books.

6. Gilbert, Elizabeth (2015). Big Magic: Creative Living Beyond Fear. New York: Riverhead Books.
7. Stewart, Tenae (2020). The Modern Witch's Guide To Magickal Self-Care: 36 Sustainable Rituals For Nourishing Your Mind, Body, and Intuition. New York: Skyhorse Publishing.
8. Stewart, Tenae (2020). The Modern Witch's Guide To Magickal Self-Care: 36 Sustainable Rituals For Nourishing Your Mind, Body, and Intuition. New York: Skyhorse Publishing.
9. Bernstein, Gabrielle. (2019). Super Attractor: Methods For Manifesting a Life Beyond Your Wildest Dreams. Carlsbad, CA: Hay House, Inc.
10. Bernstein, Gabrielle. (2019). Super Attractor: Methods For Manifesting a Life Beyond Your Wildest Dreams. Carlsbad, CA: Hay House, Inc.

There can be joy in every moment if we allow ourselves to find it.

You are the wind
You are the light of the sun
You are the trees and the tides of the seas

The convergence within you is palpable
Yet without you reaching inside to draw the whole together,
None will overcome the raging of life's storm

Be swift in your awareness of this truth
Own your power to become all that is
And with this great emergence of energy, may the harmonious peace of existence emerge

Chapter Six

Finding Your Own Proportional Balance

As I sit here typing this manuscript, I'm overlooking the mountains and the rooftops of the city, candles ablaze and crystals surrounding my desk. I'm in my element. I've set aside the time to go deep within my thoughts, drag out the depths of my truth, put it down on the page, and create. I've established this time as a space to feel connected to myself and grounded with the surrounding landscape. This regular practice helps me feed my soul with the elemental energies that I need most, and this is something you can create in your own life now as well.

We've worked our way through the specifics of each element to where you probably felt a clear connection to some over others. Perhaps you've found yourself in some activities mentioned or the characteristics of these energies. Now, it's time to understand how you can establish a sense of balance from the proper blend of elemental energies that's uniquely meant for your lifestyle.

Just as I create routines to accommodate the spiritual within me, the creative spark that needs to emerge, and the burning desire to produce something from nothing, you are now perfectly primed to bring your own energies together in a meaningful way. It doesn't have to be through crystals and candles, but perhaps you can discover what brings you joy and let that shape your days. Remember, being in balance means you're in alignment with your own true nature, not achieving some outside idea of doing a bit of everything equally. If you feel in harmony with yourself, you'll show up better in your life and feel a greater sense of fulfillment each day without worrying about where you're headed.

Look at how each element aligns with your best self, so you'll be able to find the balance that works for you and start piecing that together step by step. You'll likely need a lot more of one or two energies than the rest. Those will be the ones that most closely align with how you perceive the world and choose to approach it. We all perceive things differently. Not all of us think things through thoroughly. Some of us feel incredibly deeply, and others of us live practically. There's no wrong answer for how you should show up in your life. Trust that following your heart will lead you down the right path.

This chapter will look at how you can now establish your energy balance by working with the elements proportionally. This can be in terms of your time, actions, resources, and effort you put into each one. You know now what the benefits can be from each element individually, but when you put them together into a cohesive mix in your life, the outcome is powerful. For example, you'll be able to ground your energy in the heat of the moment and not let the outside world provoke you into reactions you wouldn't normally choose. You could end up seizing the moment of a great opportunity because you already know exactly what feels aligned in your heart. The potential for your life becomes limitless, and it's all possible because you have equipped yourself with the elemental energies you need.

Besides the overall implications, your days can become more meaningful and heart-centered. You can start developing rituals and routines that support your continued growth and nourishment. For example, if you know that it's really important for you to feel grounded and centered most of the time, then you can build in daily practices such as meditation or nature walks to give you the feeling that you crave. The way you live should be an outward expression of who you know yourself to be on the inside. If you know yourself to be incredibly creative, then you can lean into your water energy as much as you can. Being someone who always plans, you may further develop a Sunday routine to prepare for each week or develop a monthly time to look at upcoming plans. Developing your habits, routines, and practices around the elements that most deeply resonate with you make your life a complete manifestation of your unique energy. You'll essentially be conveying the beauty of who you are in each moment through the energies that you embody.

The key is to become more aware of who you really are so that you're operating from a place of personal power as you move through life. It's up to you to decide how much of each element corresponds to your unique setpoints and when to make adjustments. Otherwise, you'll be following someone else's idea of a successful balance which could lead to a result you actually don't want. That's why it's time to look a bit more closely at yourself. Think about which energies make you feel most like yourself, which ones make you feel alive and happy, and which ones make you feel you're living your best life. Everything will feel in sync when you've found the right mix, and your life will flow more smoothly.

YOUR DOMINANT ENERGY

To clarify where your energy proportions lie, it's best to start with your dominant energy. We all have an element that we're most connected with and comfortable invoking most of the time. If you're intuitive and wear your heart on your sleeve, then you're probably a dominant water energy. If you're always in your head thinking about new ideas or solutions to problems, then it's the air element for you. Knowing where your natural default lies will give you a good indication of the elemental energy you need to lean into to feel like your best self.

If you've got an element in mind that you really feel drawn to and that most resembles who you'd like to be, but for whatever reason you've been neglecting or holding back on, then it's time to realize that and make some changes. This is your chance to not only be clear about your natural tendencies, but also about the person you know you want to be in the next season of your life. There's always room for change and renewal. Just because you may have been doing things a certain way all along doesn't mean you need to continue doing them that way. Dig deep and intuitively follow the path to where your energy really wants to go. Your heart won't steer you in the wrong direction, so if you haven't been listening to it a great deal yet, then it's a good time to start.

As you begin, you can look at several factors to identify where your dominant energy lies. First, you can take your astrological sign and determine which of the four elements it's aligned to. Each zodiac sign corresponds to either earth, air, fire, or water, and some are more heavily dominated by them than others. Taurus, Virgo, and Capricorn encompass the earth signs.[1] Air signs include Gemini, Libra, and Aquarius. The fire signs are Aries, Leo, and Sagittarius. Then, the water element signs are Cancer, Scorpio, and Pisces.[2] Connecting your sign to its corresponding element could give you a clue into where your natural energy flows based on the typical personality of that sign.

For example, I am a Libra, which is an air sign. I'm always thinking about new ideas or projects and planning out how to accomplish them. It makes me happy to be in planning mode and achieve all kinds of schemes and dreams. So, for me, my sign accurately shows that I do heavily lean into the air element. However, even though this may be the default for me, I consider my fire and water energies to be very strong as well. I know this because I've done the work to get to know myself better, see the patterns throughout my life, and key in on how I approach the world. So the air element may not be highly dominant over the other energies in my case, even though I tend toward that one the most.

As I just mentioned, another way to consider where your dominant energy lies is to look at your life's journey and identify the key pieces that stand out to you. Have you spent most of your life living artistically? Do you like adventure, travel, and discovering new things? Have you always kept to yourself, played it safe, or lived practically? Think about how you've shown up in your life until this point and how comfortable you've been with the way your journey has progressed. You should be able to pinpoint a general tendency that you lean toward based on all that we've discussed. Let your intuition be your guide as you look at all your experiences, determine where you have put your priorities, and how that has felt for you.

Let me give you another example. Maybe you've lived a very adventurous life. Perhaps you've traveled the world, worked in different jobs, and made friends everywhere you've been. You have the mindset that you should seize every moment and experience life fully. So, as someone who dives into life and loves being active in whatever you're pursuing, you would be a dominant fire energy. Your lifestyle tips heavily toward that summer season of liveliness and activity, and it's clear by the experiences you've had that this is where your heart truly lies.

Given that example, I want you to try this for yourself. Look at the career you've chosen, the people you associate with, the places you've gone, and even what you usually say "yes" or "no" to doing. Write them down and see if you can place them into a general lifestyle choice according to the elements. Do you approach life as a heady, wise air element? Are you a mindful, grounded earth energy? Will you likely go all-in on whatever you're working on to get things done? Or perhaps you like to go with the flow and see where life takes you? The memories that have shaped your life, especially the most vivid ones, can be some vital glimpses into your soul's natural alignment. They've been leaving breadcrumbs for you to find your way back to your highest state of being. It's time to pay attention to those breadcrumbs and acknowledge where your heart and soul really lie.

And then finally, come back to who you are at your core. After you've looked at your zodiac sign and you've gone through your life experiences, it's time to go deeper into your personality traits. Make a list of all the traits and characteristics you believe you possess without judgment. Look at the list and group the traits based on the elements they connect with. See where you are most inclined to steer your energy. For instance, if you describe yourself in mostly feminine terms such as creative, intuitive, or kind, then you can consider water to be your dominant energy. If you write things like deep thinker, knowledgeable, a good listener, or decisive, then air would be the natural tendency for you. Traits such as driven, determined, active, adventurous, or social, would put you in the fire energy camp. Then, things such as practical, down to earth, a nature lover, or meditative would suggest an earth energy for you.

Deep down, you know where your natural default lies, and it's important to be accepting of this so that you're not always fighting against the current of who you are. We're not doing this exercise to put you in a box and create more labels around who you are. The point here is to increase your conscious awareness around your best states of being. It's not to boost your ego, prove that you're better at something than anyone else, or to establish you in any one group of people. You are who you are, and that is unique to anyone else. Understanding your primary elemental energy is only a means to encourage alignment, not a way to put constraints on you or hold you back from being anything else.

That being said, the more you resist who you are, the more you create friction. Life doesn't have to be hard unless you make it that way. It's okay for things to come easily for you and for life to feel like a blessing most, if not all, of the time. The choice to experience things in your most balanced, aligned state will remove the barriers to your happiness and create an endless flow that brings you much more peace. Every time you choose your most authentic self over what the outside world dictates for you, you elevate your vibration and connect more strongly to the ideal version of you. So take the time now to embrace your natural element. Appreciate how it has helped you enjoy life or how it can from now on. See the strengths in who you are and choose a peaceful existence over any resistance you may have felt in the past.

WHERE YOU MAY BE LACKING

Next, it's time to acknowledge which elements you feel are lacking in your life. Doing this will help you reestablish a baseline in every aspect of yourself so you can maintain a certain level of satisfaction and comfort. Take some time to identify the areas you feel depleted in or need to work on in order to bring your energy back up. It could be in terms of self-care, using your water energy to make you feel nourished, or even giving yourself the attention you deserve. Perhaps you're not attending to your fire energy currently and that you haven't really set any big goals for yourself in a while. So it could be time to get out of your comfort zone.

Pinpoint the areas where you may not have been devoting enough time by leaning into your intuition. Get out a journal and allow yourself to explore what is working and what isn't. Be open to whatever comes out and be willing to just observe your thoughts and feelings. Pay close attention to the underlying emotions connected to the outward expression of things. For example, if you're unhappy with your job at the moment, then it could be from the lack of passion or inspiration you feel underneath. That may uncover a depleted water energy that needs to be brought back up to a higher level so you can once again feel enthusiastic about what you're working towards.

When you identify what is missing in your life, you can do a better job of fixing the problem and not letting it fester. Putting a metaphorical bandaid over something that's causing issues and trying to move on from it actually diminishes our personal power to improve our lives. It only holds us in a state of denial and numbness to not address what needs improvement. We have to be brave enough to first see where the gaping holes exist and prepare ourselves to deal with them consciously in order for actual progress to occur. It's only when we finally tear the bandaid off and see what's lacking that we can step into our power and make the adjustments to get back into alignment once again.

So with that knowledge, you may have to spend a bit more time in the beginning to fill your cup in areas that have been lacking. If it's your water energy, for instance, then maybe you take a couple of months to immerse yourself in creative pursuits. You could sign up for an art class, do some photography on the weekends, explore some local museums, or even discover a new sense of style with your wardrobe. After you feel renewed in a creative sense, it's time to find a reasonable level to sustain your water energy without letting it dip so low that you feel it lacking again.

Essentially, what we want to do here is to bring all of your energy levels back up to an adequate level before we decide what the standard will become for you. At some point, you will have some typical proportions for how you integrate each elemental energy into your life, and I'll walk you through how to figure that out in the next section. First, though, you have to get everything to a point where you feel somewhat in-tune with yourself and comfortable with your current state of being. After you do this rebalancing process, that's when you can give yourself a baseline for lifelong energetic success.

ESTABLISHING PROPORTIONS THAT WORK FOR YOU

The best way to create a sustainable way of aligning with your elemental energies is to establish your baseline energetic proportions. Think about this in terms of a pie chart where each elemental energy has a different size slice of the pie. For some people, one particular element may take up a much larger portion of the pie than the others. Yet, other people may have each element more equally distributed among their pie slices, and that's perfectly okay. We're all going to have different variations on how we need to be present in our lives. It's good to have this consistent understanding of what your baseline slices look like. Having this will make you better equipped to create more continuous alignment in your life.

Plus, depending on the season of life you're in, you have more conscious control over how you might need to adjust each piece of your energetic pie without getting completely oversaturated in one area or depleted in another. You'll be able to prioritize and rebalance based on what's most needed. We do this through always keeping in mind our dominant energy and giving ourselves enough proportions of the others to maintain a certain level of satisfaction with each one.

Let's give this a try for your own energetic baseline. Use any resources you have available to you to create a pie chart. You can use your favorite software, draw it in a notebook or journal, or even get creative with paper cutouts and art materials. Start with an entire circle that signifies your whole self and divide it into eight equal parts. You will place all four elements into the circle based on how many slices they each require.

Place your dominant element into the circle first by determining how much of the whole that element should regularly take up in your life. For example, you may decide that you have a great deal of water energy. You may feel like your best self when you're leaning into that element about half of the time. This amount could be based on the time you need to work on creative projects, how much impact your emotions have on you, or even the time you devote to taking care of yourself and others. You can just make a rough estimate here, as this is only a starting point from which you'll be able to test things out. From here, you would color in four slices of your pie chart to correspond with the half that you designated toward your water energy.

Then, you would move onto the other energies and place those on the chart. Suppose you decide you need more earth energy to ground you after being enveloped in water energy most of the time. In that case, there would then be two slices left over which you could choose to split evenly between air and fire energy to give you a nice bit of both. The way you divide up your chart will depend on how heavily you lean toward your dominant energy, how intense your secondary energy is, and the extent to which you need the other two energies.

When you're filling in this baseline chart, always look at your natural tendencies to make conclusions. Once you place an energy in your chart with a certain number of slices, ask yourself if it really makes sense for how you want to be living and if it intuitively feels good to you. Is most of your time really spent feeling like the greatest section of the pie? Do you feel good about where you've placed the other elements in terms of how much they're going to support you? If something feels like it's not quite right, then experiment with it until you feel like it's a good enough mix to get you started. Nothing is set in stone here. We're just looking for a reasonable expectation of where to start applying these energies in your life.

The next step is to fill in some activities, rituals, and practices that fit nicely into these sections of the whole. Start once again with the largest section, since that should be the easiest to figure out. Think about what day-to-day activities would fulfill the energetic need for whichever element is your largest proportion. It could be anything from doing a twenty-minute morning meditation to sitting outside for five minutes in the evenings or even checking on the progress you've made toward your goals at the end of the workday. Get a handful of ideas for your dominant energy, and then write the specific activities inside the largest section of your pie chart. Repeat this process for intermittent things that you can do as well, such as seasonal trips, meetups, or annual activities. Then, you're going to do this entire process again for every other elemental energy section of your chart until it's filled in.

When you've got it completed, you should have a full pie divided up into four sections. Each one will have a handful of activities that feel very connected and aligned with that energy for you. There will be some daily activities and some that are sporadic, seasonal, or happening over larger periods of time. Your largest section should have the most activities placed within it that enable you to draw upon this energy most often in various ways. This is the section where everything should feel like your most authentic self and bring you a great deal of joy when you do these activities. Then, your second largest section should be one that you pay a lot of attention to also, as this one helps you keep your balance on most days. If you're feeling like you're leaning too heavily into your dominant energy, then you should have plenty of suggested activities within your secondary element to maintain a reasonable balance on any day.

Now, this chart is going to be a starting point for you to build on and adjust as you get to know yourself better. Basically, you can use it as a guide to check in and see if you're spending your time and energy in the places that keep you feeling whole. You may even decide to create a ritual around checking in with your energy and intuitively sensing where there may be any misalignment or need to readjust. You could create an end-of-the-week wind-down time where you observe the past week and prepare time on the weekend to fill in any energetic gaps. Maybe you're interested in developing a waning moon or new moon ritual where you go within to see what to shift, heal, and transform with new intentions for the next cycle of life.

No matter how you choose to integrate these energetic proportions into your life, at least start with time to try out this baseline with a few key activities. Give yourself space to readjust your state of being and then check in. You'll know something isn't working if you feel uneasy, lacking, or if you experience any lower-level emotions like stress or anxiety. Those are signs that something is still off-balance, and it may be time to reevaluate your pie chart to see where to make changes. You probably won't get the right mix of energetic proportions right off the bat, so be gentle with yourself as you implement and look for the right composition for you.

TESTING OUT YOUR ENERGETIC PROPORTIONS

Using your energetic pie chart as a roadmap to create more balance in your life, you'll see patterns of what is working and what isn't. Write everything down so that you can make adjustments as needed. Take everything that stands out to you as a signal that you may need to adjust some energy and either lean more heavily into one aspect or pull back, depending on how you feel. For instance, if you find that you're only spending an eighth of your time on self-care, and you still feel overworked, then maybe your water energy needs to be bumped up closer to a quarter of your time. That could look like getting an extra hour of sleep every night, staying in more on the weekends, and having more casual days with friends and family over packing your calendar completely full.

You'll have to see where you stand now compared to what you'd like your elemental energies to look like ideally. At first, there will most likely be a great deal of changes that need to be made as you keep track of and pay more attention to the way you feel. Just acknowledging that these changes need to occur is an enormous step in the right direction. It means that you're now more conscious of how you actually want to be living. The more awareness you can bring to your reality, the better off you'll be to create the life you want now and in the future.

The major goal here, as you test out your energetic proportions, is to get to a place where you can maintain contentment with each elemental aspect of yourself. You want to, mostly, live in a higher vibration that keeps you connected with yourself, your passions and purpose, your bliss, and your truth. When we feel depleted in any one area, that's when lower-level vibrations set in and we can develop mindsets and emotions that prevent us from being our best selves. It also blocks us from manifesting all the abundance that we can create in our lives. We have to get ourselves back into alignment energetically to be a better attractor for the abundance that the universe wants to send our way. When we're energetically aligned, we're much more inclined to recognize that abundance and appreciate it.

So it's perfectly okay to set aside some time to test things out in your life. Get a sense of how things are flowing once you use your initial pie chart. It's okay if you get into a cycle where things need to lean more heavily in one direction, but do your best to come back to your pie chart as your baseline and see how that works for you. If you're comfortable with the proportions you're setting, then you have a choice in deciding how long you'll stay in those default energy settings. You get to decide when everything needs to be reset and refreshed. Plus, you get to dictate if you want to transform yourself completely and lean into a whole new side of who you are. The options are endless, but you are now in the driver's seat with greater awareness and clarity for what brings you closer to your highest self.

BRINGING ALL OF THE ELEMENTS TOGETHER

To bring these new insights together, just know that these energies have been within you this whole time. They're part of who you are and part of who you will become. You are not invoking anything different in your life. You are only more conscious about how to do it now and how much you need. The answer to those questions is going to depend on who you know yourself to be at your core and the lifestyle you are now choosing to live as you move into your future self. Every moment is a chance to make an energetic choice that aligns with the person you want to be. Have a bad day at work and need to reset? You can tap into your earth energy. Need more clarity around whether to say "yes" or "no" to something? Your air element will connect you to your most authentic self and give you the wisdom to make an aligned choice.

These elements are the tools to build a life that's completely in tune with your own rhythm and the seasonal cycles that you want in your life. You know now how to effectively balance your masculine and feminine sides to create peace from within. Life can happen "from" you now as you manifest the perspective you want instead of happening "to" you. Stop for a minute and think about the incredible power in that statement. You are the master of your own destiny because energy is emanating from you to shape your reality.

The more you get to know yourself and practice these activities, the better you'll be at releasing the expectations and limitations of the world around you and coming back to your own personal awareness. It's just a matter of setting the intention to be more mindful of your energy and following it regularly as you show up in life. Danielle LaPorte says, "Awareness is realizing that our life could always be better. Growth is doing what it takes to make it better. When we choose the positive over the negative, liberation over repression, truth over illusion, we become real creators."[3] This is my hope for you as we culminate this journey together and allow you to cultivate this growth in your own life. Be the creator that your soul already knows you to be.

Your present and future are in your hands to shape from a place of knowing yourself, your heart-centered intentions, and your joy. When you tap into these regularly through the energy cycles that we've discussed, then everything else becomes much less significant and possibly even melts away. The four elements are your gateway to achieving this moment-to-moment happiness and lifting yourself up to a high enough consciousness level to see life working in your favor.

Invoke earth when you're ready to ground deeply into your inner world and connect with the universe that you're a part of. Invoke air when your mind may give you clarity and greater understanding of what exists and what you hope to come to pass. Choose to invoke fire to fuel you confidently toward your dreams. Finally, invoke water to feel the richness of life and replenish your soul with passion and joy. All four elements may be distinguishable by their traits and benefits, but they are all one within you. The distinctions we make between these different parts are a perception. In reality, the power lies in the compilation of all energies within you. You are one energy and all energy. You are balanced and in alignment when you dictate it is so. Being mindful of this will help you create cycles without stress or pressure, but solely out of expression for your complete self.

THE WAY FORWARD

Remember to take your journey one step at a time. If you're ready to incorporate some practices from this book and create some changes in your life, then start by asking which energy you feel most drawn to working with right now and how that might support you. Always be aware of why an action feels aligned for you or how it may get you closer to becoming your best self. Build yourself up to where you're working with all of the energies, and find a good cycle if you haven't spent time in some areas in a long time. Granting yourself grace throughout the process should be your number one priority. It takes great courage, strength, and inner knowing to make your own version of a harmonized life work. Don't beat yourself up if you fall back into some old habits. Just observe so you may choose differently next time if it serves you better.

Practice starting each day with an open heart and mind. Everything will be exactly as it needs to be if you show up prepared to see life fully and opportunistically. The universe will feel your intentions and mirror them back to you with more abundance and possibilities. This is how you become a co-creator with all of the energies working in your favor. Set the closed mind aside. Assume that your emotions are guiding you to where you're supposed to go. Focus on what you can transform through your mindset, emotions, and actions. Then, take that bird's-eye view to see yourself within a larger holistic energy, and breathe.

When in doubt, return to thankfulness to guide you. With every breath and in every moment, you can find something to be grateful for that can bring you back to happiness and harmony. Let this heart-centered energy anchor you to everything you've experienced, everything you are, and everything you're trying to create. It's all available to you with the balance of energy that's within you now. As Meik Wiking relates, "To me, the good life–a full life, a rich life– is a life both of purpose and pleasure. It is when life offers satisfaction with the present, hopes for the future, and peace with the past. Happiness is not a one-ingredient dish."[4] You are all seasons of life, all of the energy of nature and the universe, and all that remains to come. Approach the idea of balance in your life as if it already exists and you are now choosing to honor that existence and showcase it more in your life. The feeling of balance will naturally come as you shed the veil of outside expectations and more fully engage with the incredible energies that lie within.

Your inner light is ready to illuminate the path to a beautiful way of being, and it's time to follow it forward. May you take each step with curiosity in your mind, compassion in your heart, strength in your will, and calm in your soul. Know that balance is your own and in every moment, the energies of your highest and best self lie within you.

1. Determine your dominant elemental energy by looking at your life experiences, personality, and even your astrological sign.

2. Figure out which areas of your energy seem lacking and decide how much more time you'd be willing to put into them in order to feel better.

3. Create an elemental energy chart based on the proportions of energy you'd like to devote to each element regularly.

4. Implement your energy proportions through consistent activities and practices that align with each element. Track your progress and look at any patterns or signs you may find to make adjustments.

You're ready to live a life of balance, flow, and ease. Enjoy the journey!

---

1. Regan, Sarah (2021). "An Introduction To The 4 Elements & What They Say About Each Zodiac Sign." [Blog Article]. Retrieved in April 2022, from

https://www.mindbodygreen.com/articles/the-4-zodiac-elements.
2. Regan, Sarah (2021). "An Introduction To The 4 Elements & What They Say About Each Zodiac Sign." [Blog Article]. Retrieved in April 2022, from https://www.mindbodygreen.com/articles/the-4-zodiac-elements.
3. LaPorte, Danielle. (2014). The Desire Map: A Guide To Creating Goals With Soul. Boulder, CO: Sounds True, Inc.
4. Wiking, Meik. (2019). The Art of Making Memories: How to Create and Remember Happy Moments. New York: William Morrow.

Alignment is a state of being that only you can feel for yourself.

Download your FREE Elemental Energy Planner Pages and Tarot Card Spreads!

Plan each week so you feel your best every day! Use these **FREE daily and weekly prompt pages** to align with your intentions and create balance by planning the energetic activities, practices, and rituals that match the energy you need most in your life.

Go to:

http://authorkristenking.com/elementalplannerpages

To get your copy of the pages and start creating more alignment in your days now.

Get 20% Off The Personal Retreat Pack That Accompanies This Book!

With this personal retreat package you can plan seasonal, elemental cycles that help you grow and reach your next level goals while also feeling in balance and at peace with your life.

Go to:

**http://authorkristenking.com/retreat
And use the code: BOOKLOVE**

To get all of the guided retreat videos, workbook pages, and tarot spreads you need to put together your personal elemental retreat at home for 20% off.

About The Author

Kristen is an author, conscious living coach, and spiritual creative. She understands moving through life checking all of the boxes and living for the next accomplishment, yet still feeling misaligned and yearning for more. Once she gave herself the space to go within and connect with who she truly was, Kristen found the balance that already existed inside of her and the fulfillment that she could create for herself.

Combining her many years as a Project Management Professional (PMP), her background in art, architecture, and design, experience as a Certified Professional Coach (CPC), and a Certified Chakra Healing Practitioner (CCHP), she now supports other multi-passionate, heart-centered souls in building a conscious life. She believes that every aspect of our lives should be a deliberate and soul-connected means of fulfillment, joy, and growth. These days Kristen spends most of her time writing and creating programs to inspire the soul, empower the mind, and motivate the body toward manifesting every part of the intentional life we're drawn to living.

When not writing, creating, or coaching, she's enjoying the hygge of her home by snuggling up next to a cozy fire with her family and calico cat, sipping on a home blend of Rooibos tea, plentiful candles lit nightly, and jazz playing softly in the background. She loves to lose herself in afternoons taking photographs, diving into spiritual books, or charging crystals by the light of the moon.

For more from the author and to find her books, programs, and offerings, go to:

http://authorkristenking.com

Share Your Thoughts

If you enjoyed reading this book and found inspiration from it, then you could help others by leaving a review online. Your thoughts would be greatly appreciated and may lead someone to begin or expand their journey of self-awareness in order to spread further light in the world. Sending beautiful energy and gratitude your way.

Express your truth.
Honor your journey.

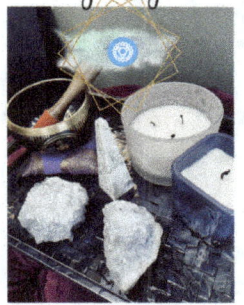

www.ingramcontent.com/pod-product-compliance
Lightning Source LLC
Chambersburg PA
CBHW071235070526
44583CB00017B/2185